LIFE,
LIBERTY AND THE
PURSUIT OF ANYTHING

LIFE, LIBERTY AND THE PURSUIT OF ANYTHING

Edward Quiros, MD MBA FACS

Copyright © 2019 by Edward Quiros, MD MBA FACS.

Library of Congress Control Number: 2019910601
ISBN: Hardcover 978-1-7960-4862-9
       Softcover 978-1-7960-4861-2
       eBook 978-1-7960-4860-5

All rights reserved. No part of this book may be reproduced or transmitted in any form or by any means, electronic or mechanical, including photocopying, recording, or by any information storage and retrieval system, without permission in writing from the copyright owner.

Any people depicted in stock imagery provided by Getty Images are models, and such images are being used for illustrative purposes only.
Certain stock imagery © Getty Images.

Print information available on the last page.

Rev. date: 07/29/2019

To order additional copies of this book, contact:
Xlibris
1-888-795-4274
www.Xlibris.com
Orders@Xlibris.com

CONTENTS

Author's Note xi
Foreword xiii

LIFE

Accidental Tourist 1
Coffee Break 5
Adoption...10
Apocalypse...16
Bills..19
Casino Life 22
Eulogy 26
Friendship and Friends...29
Genealogy 32
Going to Church..36
Reunions 40
Code Blue Above the Clouds 44
What's in a Name? 49
Surrogacy 53
Weight Control 57
Professions 62
Inheritance 65
Smartphones...68
Karaoke 72
Lotto 76
Sleep..80
Genealogy 84
Medical and Surgical Missions 88

Television 93
Movie Houses 97
Rivers 100

LIBERTY

Diversity 105
Plagiarism 108
PC (Better Known as Politically Correct) 112
Voting 115
Drugged 118
Political Parties 125
Health Care 129
Term Limits 134
Taxes 138
Crime 142
Doctors 146
Charitable Organizations 150
Weather 154
The Fourth Estate 158
Marriage 161
History Revisited 165
Mentorship 168
Change and Leadership 171
Identity 174

PURSUIT OF ANYTHING

Fishing 181
Golf 186
Cruising 191
Driving 194
Dancing 197
Collecting 201
Cooking 204
Keeping Time 208
Bird-Watching 211

Shopping 214
Moving 218
Aging.. 223
Dining 226
Wine Tasting 230
House 234
Birthdays.. 238
Bookworm.. 241
Insurance.. 244

For my Family and my Friends.

Author's Note

I am not a writer. Or an author of novels or essays. It always discourages me to see so many authors or writers, some established, others just attempting to make a name for themselves every time I enter a bookstore and see thousands and thousands of titles of novels or books or whatever the writer thinks it is worth writing about. Some new editions, others neatly arranged in that heap called bargain purchases. It immediately put a stop to my idea of putting what I think is a subject that must be indelible , of every day events that people talk about after seeing it on TV or coming across in a page of a local or national newspaper. Something like Charles Krauthammer seminal essays in Things That Matter, Andy Rooney's astute observations in Common Sense. Or the provocative articles in humorist Dave Barry's I am Not Making This Up.

   But growing older in age and with the remaining future not so distant anymore, the impulse and the courage to tell anyone who is interested in what you have to say becomes convulsive as a magma wanting to erupt from the bowels of the earth's core. That is why these essays compiled and culled from the files of what I have kept these years writing editorials in magazines, from applications to a graduate school I never finished and received a diploma, and from other sources the names I can't recall, from recent and contemporaneous events onerously repeated by pundits and so-called experts, became bound in a form you are holding today. The ideas may be past but still relevant. They might be current and dissecting them with the pros and cons of opinions providing the diversity we strive for. I do not claim originality in the subjects I write about. They might not be original but I have burnished them with a different patina the reader never thought of colorizing. The research of some of the data was done via websites, different articles read, speeches made, my notes and recollections and some older versions of articles I have written in some newsmagazines. For privacy reasons, I have changed the names in one essay in particular as I was not successful in communicating with the persons despite attempts at doing so. I have also to the best of my ability adhered to the fair use doctrine using some data or quotations in some of my essays.

In any case, I hope it is while your time, effort, and your trip to the bookstore to come up and peruse what is in your hands.

Foreword

My acquaintance with Edward E. Quiros, MD, MBA, FACS, FICS, started in 1981 while I was president of the Society of Philippine Surgeons in America (SPSA), a professional fellowship of US-trained Filipino-American surgeons practicing in the United States, established in 1972.

Ed and I seem to have taken amusing parallel, sometimes convergent, paths in life. We are both married to physicians, both surgical specialists, he in hand and upper extremity surgery, and I in cardiac and thoracic surgery. We are both fellows of the American College of Surgeons and the International College of Surgeons. He was SPSA president in 2002–2004; I was twenty-one years earlier. In 1975, I was appointed by SPSA founding president Hernan M. Reyes, MD, FACS, the inaugural editor of the *Philippine Surgeon*, SPSA's official publication, a stint I held for twenty-two and a half years. Ed succeeded me as editor in 1998. I was named website director in 2006 and commissioned to create and manage the SPSAtoday website. In 2010, Ed became the website director, a position he still holds. We both reside in Las Vegas, both now retired and re-tired, going on medical missions abroad, giving medical lectures at symposia, and both book authors with the same publisher. Those beguiling similarities and common interests inspired me to readily accept Ed's gracious invitation to write the foreword for this book.

Ed's notable innate humility dominates his unpretentious demeanor, in spite of his countless achievements, as a surgeon, as a respected medical leader, lecturer, writer, a wonderful husband to Corazon Quiros, MD (OB-Gyn), also a former SPSA president (2016), and as a great father to their two children. But there is nothing ordinary about Ed. Underneath that shell of selflessness and quiet mien is a truly learned man, with admirable wisdom, a great sense of humor, superior intellect, and a library of knowledge beyond medicine.

This book reflects the man and his views of the world we live in today, expressed in a succinct methodical manner, on topics ranging from professionalism, golf, taxes, crime, to bird-watching, and more. The rhetorical parallelism in this informative book is self-evident of the author's strategy to simplify serious and deep social and philosophical verities for us to reflect on, to be a part of us forever. The entertaining erudite style and magnificent essence of this writing are glazed with inherent truths and pragmatic realities that the reader is to be ushered into a recognizable self-realization. The meaningful words in Ed's writings are truly the radiance of wisdom, brilliant lights to be soon naked before us from behind today's distracting human clouds, waiting for the readers to behold and savor.

I find this well-written book, *Life, Liberty, and Pursuit of Anything*, a labor of love by Dr. Ed Quiros, to be most creatively refreshing and skillfully entertaining. It reminds me of life in this complex world of wonders and how to live it well, with a smile.

Philip S. Chua
Philip S. Chua, MD, FACS, FPCS
Cardiac Surgeon Emeritus, NWI
26 May 2019
Las Vegas, Nevada

Life

Accidental Tourist

In the 1988 award-winning movie *The Accidental Tourist* adapted from Anne Tyler's book, Macon Leary (played by William Hurt) withdrew from the world following the death of his son, moved in with his sister to recuperate from a broken leg, interacted with middle-aged intellectuals who gradually caused him to come out of his self-protective shell. In today's environment, an accidental tourist may have taken on a new meaning or turn when someone who is in need of care finds that he or she becomes not only a patient but a contemporaneous tourist as well in some foreign land, a far outreach from staying or even withdrawing from a world he or she has grown accustomed to. With so many that are aware of this newfound phenomenon, this has spawned a new industry called medical tourism. In the United States in 2007, there were 750,000 Americans who went to other countries for health care. In 2017, it is estimated that more than 1.4 million more sought medical care and attention in various countries where the procedures in this country were much more expensive than it is in other health care systems in the world.

Many Americans who do not have health insurance and even if they do because of the recent Affordability Care Act known by its common name Obamacare, who are self-employed and are too well-off for any kind of medical assistance, or those whose procedures are not covered by their existing health insurance and have to fund the operation themselves, find that they can save a bundle by having their surgery and medical care overseas. Consider that a coronary bypass surgery costs between $70,000 to $133,000 in the United States as against $7,000 in India or $11,500 to $17,500 in the Philippines, or that a hip or knee replacement runs between $33,000 to $57,000 as against $7,500 in Malaysia, $8,000 in Poland or $7,200 in Colombia, it is thus easy to understand why medical travelers will cross the ocean for these rack-rate procedures. A husband of my niece had his cataract surgery performed overseas and convinced his brother to do the same. The health care industry, large employers and insurance companies, and now some medical schools are taking interest, with some consternation and skepticism about where all these will eventually lead to. The arrangements are generally made by concierge or broker services who help find the appropriate hospitals, physicians, and surgeons who will perform the operation, the pre- and post-operative stay at hotels or resorts, travel arrangements and other handholding amenities.

Several countries in the Middle East, South America, Eastern Europe, the Caribbean, and Southeast Asia have locked on this burgeoning commerce which according to Bloomberg quoting PwC consulting firm will reach $125 billion by 2021. Two years ago in 2016, 14 million people spent an estimated $68 billion on medical tourism as people become more comfortable with having their medical care and surgeries abroad. The United States remains the primary source of patients for the most popular procedures performed and health issues that include ophthalmology, orthopedics, cardiac and cosmetic surgery, liver and kidney transplants, and dentistry.

While the cost of health care expenditure remains the driving force for many to seek medical services in other worldwide markets, there are other factors to consider when one decides to travel long distances to avail of its potential advantages. While the medical facilitators, some regulated, others not, by existing government agencies, arrange and direct patients to the most suitable hospitals, hotel and resort accommodations, specialist physicians and surgeons sometimes foreign-trained and qualified as their American and European counterparts, there remains doubt and apprehension about the safety and quality of care these medical nomads will get should they have the services at home. Are there malpractice suits for foreign hospitals and doctors when unexpected results and complications happen after they return to the United States? Will US doctors be willing to take care of these complications as a result of foreign doctors' and the hospital's intervention in the delivery and performance of these procedures? One way to allay the fears and erase the doubts and apprehensions in medical tourism—the medical staff and the hospitals in the global medical tourism market must be accredited by the Joint Commission International, a global arm of the JCAHO, which accredits and makes sure that US hospitals meet stringent and specific standards. In 2017, 800 facilities were accredited worldwide with 20 percent more added to the rolls every year. While accreditation does not necessarily ensure good care, it does convey evidence of safety.

One trend not highlighted or vetted in some studies conducted about medical tourism is the ethnic preference for destination in medical travel. In a 2011 study published in the *Journal of General Medicine*, looking at hospitals outside the United States, it was found that persons would rather return to the country they were originally from or from the nation of their birth. This simply implies that Hispanics and Latinos prefer going to South America or Asians to Asian countries, Mexicans to Mexico, for their outbound medical services, while the expectation that I, being born in a country across the pond, would return to my country of origin if I needed medical care would probably not happen even with the verifiable evidence of excellence in the facilities, the quality of health care by those who provide them, and the advanced technology and equipment, even if the travel and the recuperation includes visits to historical sites and pristine beaches and the well-known hospitality of the people.

Macon Leary was not as fortunate as me. You see, I did not lose my two kids, my whole family is here, and I worked long enough to have my Social Security and my Medicare card and health insurance free.

(Adapted from *Philippine Surgeon* editorial July 8, 2008 and updated October 2018)

Medicine also disregards national boundaries.

Irving Langmuir, Nobel Prize winner, physicist, and chemist

Coffee Break

In 1984, a commercial jingle that says "The best thing on waking up is Folger's in your cup" was aired mostly on television to promote Folger's, a coffee brand by a company of the same name founded in 1850 in San Francisco, California. It no longer runs now. It has been thirty-four years since the company and its precursors initiated the advertisement that made it, in the early 1990s, the largest-selling ground coffee in the United States, where more than 400 million or 83 percent of adults consume an average a cup of joe daily, making the country the leading consumer of coffee in the world. Not even the fictional Juan Valdez, who has appeared in advertisements since 1958 specifically marketing coffee only grown and harvested on the slopes of Colombia, can displace the aroma brought by the Folger's commercial.

    Over the years, the practice of looking first and having a drink of the beverage early in the morning has morphed into a culture that has enveloped everyone else and resulted in coffee shops, houses, bars, and even parts of offices that have become social headquarters where people show up and go. Early in the morning, it is a jolt of caffeine it provides, a perceived necessity to start up a day. It is one reason why most Americans, who now consider drinking coffee as a pastime, drink coffee as a pick-me-up following a nighttime spell. Although it has been said that early morning coffee is not the best time because it may interfere with cortisol production and it is best to wait for an hour, this suggestion to most people is a heresy not to be invoked or followed. Any time of the day and all the seasons of the year, a warm brew imbibed or sipped is a recognition of being part of a progressive civilization. After all, the earliest reference to coffee in America was in 1668 by the English colonizers, and coffee was made popular in the early eighteenth century after the Boston Tea Party, when it was considered a patriotic duty to switch from tea to coffee. Nowadays, the coffee break has worked its way into corporate culture, where it is not considered a patriotic duty but a common practice expected whether one is a coffee drinker or not. I asked a friend of mine who happens to be a supervisor in one large firm how a trip to break room in midmorning or midafternoon for a free cup of coffee has impacted the efficiency and company relationships with the employees. She has responded that not only were the employees better because of the respect and interaction during these short intervals but she and the relationships with the company were much stronger. It is worthwhile noting that since 2012, the number of Americans drinking a cup of coffee is at its highest level.

The word "coffee" made its first appearance in the English lexicon in 1582 with the Dutch word *koffie*. The origin of coffee remains a conjecture, although the evidence points to the Islamic world, specifically Ethiopia, where the energizing effects of boiled bright-red berries by Omar, a disciple of a Moroccan Sufi mystic, resulted in a fragrant brown liquid that unusually revitalized the birds and subsequently sustained him during his exile in a desert cave. Despite the origins in Ethiopia, the country produced only a small amount of export until the twentieth century, much of it grown and produced in the northeastern part of the country. Centuries later, despite the initial bans imposed during the fifteenth century by religious leaders in the Islamic countries and later by the Catholic Church, coffee drinking spread to the rest of Europe, to the East Indies, and to the Americas. It has been widely held that even Johann Sebastian Bach composed a secular "Coffee Cantata," in which a young woman implored her disapproving father to accept her fervor to drinking the concoction.

There are four varieties of commercially available the coffee beans eventually defined based mostly on the caffeine each one contained: arabica, liberica (*barako*), Excelsior, and robusta. The latter was defined to be a cheaper coffee bean, having more caffeine than the more expensive ones, a factor in its popularity among the coffee habitués. Arabica, like robusta, tends to have a fruity, sweeter, and softer, winey taste with an acidity that is much higher. Once all the various beans are roasted, they tend to look the same. The taste, however, is different for every coffee drinker no matter what variety each one drinks. Brazil, having the first coffee plantation and turning the beverage from elite indulgence to a drink for the masses, became the world's number one producer, monopolizing and setting the high prices of coffee, resulting in other countries seeing an opening in the production of comparable or lower pricing structure. Vietnam now is the second major coffee producer in the world, second only to Brazil.

What makes people from all over the world consume an average of 2.25 billion cups of coffee each day or what the more prominent coffee shop Starbucks likely sell 2.9 billion cups a year in their stores, is based on the discovery of caffeine in the coffee bean and its purported value, uses, and all the medicinal rituals associated with it. Caffeine in coffee, a widely consumed psychoactive drug, legal and still unregulated, has been touted to provide potential health benefits, with some studies suggesting reducing the risks of developing mouth, throat, and liver cancers. Other studies have shown that coffee and its caffeine content protects against type 2 diabetes, Parkinson's disease and that its antioxidant properties significantly improve circulation to the coronaries and overall the blood flow to clogged arteries. It is even used as an enema in alternative medicine as a cleansing therapy designed to boost immunity, increase energy and treat depression, remove metals from the body, and eventually as a treatment for cancer. While there is no scientific evidence that coffee enemas are helpful in treating these conditions, there were a number of celebrities who believed and tried the non-mainstream, alternative treatment, which according to the National Cancer Institute carries significant risks.

On the other hand, there are inherent bad effects of drinking too much coffee—no, not 80–100 cups a person consumes in a day, which can result in convulsions and subsequent death—but maybe more than the average individual's 3–4 or even 10 cups a day. It has also been demonstrated that coffee containing caffeine causes insomnia, restlessness, agitation, nausea and vomiting, tachypnea, tachycardia and tachyarrhythmia, gout and headaches. Women who have fibrocystic disease have been advised to refrain from excessive coffee—more than 3–4 cups per day. Sometimes it distorts and messes up the blood sugar levels and is said to interfere with sex hormones that decreases the libido. The pendulum of the good, the bad, and the ugly of drinking this black or creamy liquid swings depending on what one believes, prefers, or experiences. But sipping coffee in reasonable amounts of not more than four 6-ounce cups of coffee per day has been shown by several studies to be one of the healthiest things one can do.

The coffee business has undergone several evolutions. One can no longer go to the groceries or coffee houses or bars without knowing the many concoctions coffee has undergone. There is the latte, the cappuccino, several ready-made coffee flavors, the Keurigs and the single-use packs, and several brands in luminous and attractive cans and containers. To attract more customers, many shops continually alter their operational schemes to include price modifications, providing Wi-Fi and social media connections, starting and maintaining loyalty cards, tapping suppliers for product components and marketing developments, and even giving or selling takeaway cups. In addition to these corporate ploys, they strive to make the coffee shops and houses bright and user friendly.

Coffee and the caffeine it contains will certainly not go away. It is here to stay for as long as the populace finds that having it early in the morning and throughout the day is a culture phenomenon not only available at home or in coffee shops, but even in mundane places such as gas stations. I was totally immersed in this culture in my younger days when the need to always have the caffeine rush in my system required that I drink more than my share of coffee to keep me going. Now in my older days, I have learned what the younger generation has found out—that an average caffeinated soda has about half the amount of a coffee cup, and that contrary to prevailing belief, a cup of tea has more caffeine than a cup of coffee. I do not drink the average 3–4 cups per day an average person in America consumes. Neither do I drink more because I no longer worship sleep or feel the attention span its absence provided me in my younger days when I needed to be awake.

I only drink one cup in the morning. And it is good to the last drop.

> *Among the numerous luxuries of the table . . . coffee may be considered as one of the most valuable. It excites cheerfulness without intoxication; and the pleasing flow of spirits which it occasions is never followed by sadness, languor or debility.*
>
> *Benjamin Franklin*
>
> *Coffee and love are best when they are hot.*
>
> *German proverb*

Adoption

My sister Josefina has been married to Ricardo, a Puerto Rican-American, for many years now. And while his name denotes that of a winged gentle creature, he never was and is. He was one of a set of twins. I still do not know to this day the name of his twin brother But we all have accepted him no matter his name is, though truth be told, we always wondered why his parents gave him that prefix to his Catalonia family surname.

Early on, my sister and Ricardo tried but she could not conceive and get pregnant. Cognizant that she comes from a family of thirteen brothers and sisters, it became frustrating afterward that even for once, she and her husband could not even have one, let alone that they exhausted all avenues to bring us a nephew or a niece. And so they resorted to a process called adoption, a maze that includes many twists and turns of which they, and even we, really don't know the beginning or the end. Though we finally learned some of what it is all about—a proposition historical in its roots that in its present form, the adapting couple assumes the parenting of the adoptee, transferring the rights and the responsibilities from the biological parents to the adopting couple. Simple as it is understood, it really has many questions to all the facets involved in the adoption process.

Being an interracial couple, they were bent on having as close to adopting someone similar to or close to what my sister dictated—that he or she would look like her, brown in skin, flat nose, maybe shorter or slightly taller that she is. Never mind that Ricardo was white in complexion, looking more Castilian than a typical Puerto Rican. They went to her country of origin in Asia, contacted an orphanage run by Catholic sisters and were initially offered a female child who had medical issues. After consulting with me, they decided to decline the offer and instead settled on a baby boy that the nuns were hoping to keep for a long time as he apparently was a healthy lovable foundling left to the orphanage by an unwed mother and a married father. Martin was brought to the United States and was immediately considered and treated a part of the family to which he has responded as his own. He is now a junior at a major university and behaves like he was a biological son along with his filiation to my sister and her husband, who continue to provide him with all the necessities of his growing up. I think that sometimes he has looked back at the possibility of the eugenics associated with his biologic parents, who were apparently well educated. My sister and her husband openly told him when he was able to comprehend that they would not be offended if in the future, Martin would look for his biological parents and why they had to give him up at the closed orphanage established and run by the Catholic nuns. I am not sure, nevertheless, whether these institutional issues of adoption ever crossed his mind, knowing that the process was meant to ensure the best interest of the child.

In the United States, adoption in this century that emerged tends to be governed by statutes and regulations that are rather comprehensive. The practice of adoption became more prevalent after World War II when illegitimate births rose threefold as sexual mores changed. Though adoption declined temporarily in the '60s and '70s, because of the government's campaign about artificial birth control and the introduction of birth control pill, federal funding for family planning to the young and the low-income population, and the legalization of abortion, it began to peak and has remained constant since the late '80s, 3 per 100 live births in a population of 300 million compared to Norway or Australia, where it is less than 1 percent per 100 relative or non-family adoptions. White, younger adolescents who have a higher level of education and who live in a two-parent environment appear to release and give up their babies to non-relatives than blacks, who come from single parents and have lower educational status and tend to receive more from their relatives and communities' informal adoption terms.

Not unlike the practice promulgated by the Codex Justinianus of Rome or the Code of Hammurabi in ancient Greece. It is well known that many of the emperors of Rome were adopted sons like Trajan, who was adopted by emperor Nerva, who in turn was adopted as his own emperor Hadrian. Bloodlines were important, and if no heir was produced as a natural born by a dynasty, adoption became the norm. This old medieval practice was abolished by the English common law, as it contradicted the customary rule of inheritance—even more so by the Napoleonic Code, which required adopters to be old (over the age of fifty) and proven to be sterile. Today, every country that permits adoption has its own rules and regulations to be followed by anyone from another nation adopting its own citizens. Intended to change the permanent status through legal and also religious means, requiring society's acceptance, adoption, whether local, national, or international, whether closed or open, arose from antiquity to what is now a burgeoning trend and practice. My wife, a practicing obstetrician and gynecologist in her heyday received from unknown couples every now and then, from all corners of the country, requests for any information she might have regarding any mother, single, adolescent or otherwise, willing to give the child for adoption. On some occasions, she facilitated a couple's adoption process.

Which brings me to our daughter Christine. She went to a parochial school until she moved to middle school and finally graduated from local public high school. Having been partially educated by the religious order of nuns and coming from a family that was involved in the many activities of the local and the diocesan parishes, she was as devout a teenager as we expected her to be. And she was going through the many requirements and steps that the church undertook to make her a complete acolyte of the faith until she went to college. And in her reading of contemporaneous periodicals, she came across the purported account of adoption and orphanages run by nuns who acted sternly and strictly, abusing in disciplining foundlings, not for the purpose of sparing the rod and spoiling the child. The part that roiled her was that supposedly, these disciples of the faith entrusted with the orphanages and the adoption process secretly carried out their modus operandi until the author of the expose wrote about it. Appalled by these accounts, which she considered betrayals by those she looked up to, she turned her back and bitterly became almost an agnostic, not believing in faith-based adoption and the orphanages run by any religious orders. She has over the years returned to her moorings after she got over her rage and belief that the system is basically good but those who carry out its tenets are not all that good and sacrosanct. The reaction she manifested brings to the fore some faulty aspects of adoption and adoption houses, where couples turn to when the reason for adopting children they might not be related to arises.

I do not know whether my relatives followed any of the legal requirements when they adopted their two children. We did not know or bother who their parents were, so none of us ever encountered them growing up, even in our adult lives. My mother, who never saw the toes of her feet except in the early days of her pregnancy, had thirteen of us, courtesy of my father. Her sister never had any children. While my relatives provided all the opportunities to their adoptees, it seemed to me that the two they adopted suffered from uncertainty about knowing their biological family, feeling a sense of betrayal of wanting to know where they came from and believing that my relatives and those that constitute the family will love them less because of their curiosity, which is one of the negative aspects and the risks of those adopted in establishing their relationships with the couple that adopt them. The health issues and medical history of their biological parents not being known to them brings an anxiety in later years, especially if the adopting couple or the adopting facility or institution do not wish to disclose or are not made aware of the information. The boy was a lovable kid growing up but wound up in muck as he grew up to be an adult, landing him in prison and subsequently killed by fellow inmates. This despite the formative care and advice that were given them. The girl was somatically different from both auntie those that adopted her. They were tall and fair-skinned. But she graduated from college and had a comfortable job afterward before she got married to a Puerto Rican native, migrated to the United States. Haven't heard from her since after she attended the funeral services of my relatives.

There are a number of reasons for adoption. But infertility remains the main reason for the individual or the couple seeking to complete the family. There are many ways to adopt especially now that the safe haven of leaving an infant at the doorstep of somebody else's home or that of the church has been outlawed. This practice has been on the upswing lately. Whether the adoption process is between related or unrelated individuals, private or intra-family, open or closed, foster care, or any other arrangements such as same-sex joint adoption, which is now legal in more than twenty-six countries, the trend continues and public perception, though it carries some unfavorable stigma, major surveys show favorable positive impressions.

International adoptions, which constitute around 15 percent of all US adoptions, bring a set of challenges and problems. These have not deterred some of the Hollywood types we read about in tabloids as we line up for the cash register in supermarkets from adopting outside the country to children or infants from countries like Russia, Romania, or even China. Think of Madonna who adopted from Madagascar, or Brad Pitt and Angelina adopting from Thailand and Africa before and after they had their natural twins. Or adopting someone of different race or color, like Sandra Bullock, who had Louis in 2010 and Laila in 2015, and Charlize Theron adopted son Jackson, a native born from South Africa in 2012. And there are some out there who are willing to adopt from a child's country of origin, slugging it out through the laws of that different country. Come to think of it, one of the present and persistent items in the 2016 Trump presidential election victory still under a cloud of investigation is the meeting at Trump Tower arranged apparently by Trump Jr. to discuss Russian adoption policies!

We (excluding my wife, who bore and carried both for nine months in her body won't cut it) had two, and did not even consider adoption. Two children were many, especially that the two of us were under different scopes of residency, hospital facilities, and schedules, although you can say we at least had two or slightly more than two occasions when we were able to have intimate relations during this time. Though I would have prefer a number sufficient to field a basketball team, having more and enjoying the perks coming from a big family, I have no qualms having my son and daughter. At the least, adoption never became a part of our vocabulary until my sister Josefina got married and eventually went through the process.

Adopting any child is a walk into the unknown.

Unknown

Apocalypse

It is almost two decades after the beginning of the third millennium. February was a leap year, and December was when the US Supreme Court put an end to the manual voting recount in Florida to determine whether George W. Bush or Albert Gore would be the president of the country. But it was not like these events that transpired in the year that everyone dubbed as Y2K are seared in the memory of the world. It is the apocalyptic prediction that the year 2000 was believed to be the end of the world, the extinction of humanity and civilization and that malfunctions and natural catastrophes would precede or accompany this worldwide phenomenon. As a consequence of this prediction, people stocked all sorts of things as a buffer to the coming holocaust including darkness, drought, and famine, even the computer crashing on the midnight of December 31. Of course, the predicted end did not occur and people expecting what was to finally happen in their lifetime breathed a sigh of relief the following morning. To this day, I still have the candles I saved for the dark night that was supposed to end my day.

People have been predicting the end of the world for thousands of years now, starting in the year 60 during what is called the Common Era (CE) to as far as 20 or more billion years from now. Predictions of the apocalypse can be religious-related or a natural event pitting both faith and science, the Old and New Testaments against the scientific community, who like the general public believes that the end would come in the form of a nuclear war, a wayward comet colliding with the earth, earthquakes, a supernova, or machinations of an artificial intelligence. While there has not been enough research into why we try to foretell these apocalyptic events, it is interesting to note the many persons who claim these various eschatological predictions variously referred to in Christian religion as Great Tribulation, Rapture, or Last Judgment are well known, some lesser than others. People like the Scottish clergyman John Cumming, Pope Innocent III, Martin Luther, Charles Manson, Spencer Percival (a British MP), Pat Robertson, or Sun Myung Moon, the founder of Unification Church, who predicted that the year 2000 would be the end of the world. The secular fascination with this phenomenon mostly in the young who have little education and lower incomes is thought by many as a diversion from the paranoia and the fear of the situation they are in and the force powerful enough to end the world and their lives. This apocalyptic theme is generally accepted by 10 to 20 percent of the world's population.

The end of the world is variously described in destructive details by those making the predictions, especially by those who are not descendants of the Abrahamic religion. Because I have more of a spiritual slant than scientific fascination with these events, I always envision the scenes depicted on the oil-on-wood triptych *The Last Judgment*, which hangs in the National Museum in Gdansk, Poland, by the German painter Hans Memling when God comes to make the final judgment. In it, God sits atop the world; St. Michael the Archangel is driving the damned to hell. The right panel shows those who are damned and the left panel shows St. Peter and the angels guiding those with pure spirits to heaven. All of the subjects are naked; the symbol of the nakedness escapes my imagination. I suppose we are ushered into this life swathed with nothing and receive judgment clothed with nothing as well. I am not sure when judgment day comes for me and whether the scale of justice as practiced by early Egyptians would be used, with the weight of my heart balancing the feather at the other end of the scale. And if the heart is much heavier than the feather, then I would not have been worthy for any afterlife the gods of the underworld inhabit.

I say the Nicene Creed recited at every mass I attend. It is a part of the rite that after several recitals, it is axiomatic to know when the recitations of the dogma and the belief systems come in. Sometimes though, doubt comes when the apocalypse mentioned in the Creed as Judgment Day comes in, like those who prophesied it was coming. Especially when I come across an article that mentions a new discovery by archaeologists of a well-preserved imprint of a prehistoric dinosaur that walked the face of the earth billions of years ago. Or that there are still thousands of stars and the planets that have not been named or discovered in the galaxy that exists in a figment of human imagination desperately seeking of any other life in the universe. If recorded civilization as is known today did not exist five thousand years before the birth of Christianity, the fact thus remains that the world or the universe was around beforehand. Reconciling science and faith leads to an intersection where the limits of the mind can't determine where both are rational and coexistent. To many, faith is the determinant then over the explanation of what transpired before and after and that the end is sure to come sometime. Not on the next day or even a thousand years later but on a day when one's life ends and the next generation following discovers that certain species or humanoids lived and survived here many years ago. They will still ask themselves whether apocalypse is real and whether it would be coming.

Bills

It all started as soon as I was able to pound on the keys of the computer. From the time I was living in the great state of Texas to where I moved after retirement five years ago to the state of Nevada, it has been a ritual for the first two weeks of every month when I return carrying the mail from the mailbox close to our house. The bills felt like an avalanche that I had to avoid and run from. But as I have been accustomed to, I pay them all immediately as soon as I open the envelopes when they arrive. The idea of putting off or postponing paying with the meager sum I am able to receive each month has always been anathema to the culture of facing up to your responsibility from the family and the country I came from. It is not always living within your means but below it sometimes, so our brood and I were able to prioritize what is important. Growing up and not having most of the time the commodity called cash was not much of a problem, just like the many in our small village, where there were only two small stores that allowed us to buy essential goods on a credit. The owner of the store listed what we bought and purchased on a chit sheet of paper, which we did as well. At the end of every month when my father's salary arrived, we came to the store to pay everything that we owed. When the bills were settled, there is that independence of not owing a debt to someone and not having that feeling of a chain hanging around your neck.

The first time I tried to transpose my concept of not owing anyone, as was customary where I came from, was in New York in

1971. Unaware of the emergence of the plastic called credit card as a form of security and payment, I tried to pay cash for the four days I was to rent a car to visit a friend from a neighboring state. The rental agent shook his head and declined my entreaties, and how was it that he preferred the credit card to the cash I was paying him with? Fortunately, another friend who was with me then rescued me from this debacle of being ignorant of the new mode of transaction in a new world. A number of years have passed back home in the Philippines when eventually credit cards issued by many financial institutions became a manner of transaction acceptable to many, if not all, large businesses as it is now half a century after I left. The ease of using credit cards for paying purchases worldwide has become a primary reason why many have monetary woes they wallow in and try to negotiate or compromise so as to preserve their credit scores. It has spawned new and different business approaches on how to rate credit worthiness and how to settle monthly or leftover debts from overspending.

From the outset, I found the value of paying my bills online. What I receive in income every month is directly deposited to an account from which the bills are paid. While I am able to open up the account I established anywhere in the world, I also opted for receiving the paper trail, which most of the time comes in behind the online monthly bill. While I have set payments to be sent for those that hit on a particular day of the month and the amount is generally the same each time, it is difficult to send those where the expenses vary a bit even if you pay what the automatic bill lists what you owe. The paper bill that comes late might have a different total sum and an additional late fee result, although the latter were waived on a few occasions that I made the call and voiced a legitimate complaint. At the end of every monthly cycle with a zero balance from all the bills I received and paid for, a short breather becomes a temporary respite until the next two weeks of the month return.

One of the few controls I have learned to institute with my wife is to forgo buying nonessentials and downsizing where we can. The other is the concept of a financial adviser-friend who told us one day that it was always better if we adopted a system of online payment. Licking and sealing an envelope plus the progressively increasing first-class postage stamps by the United Postal Service have been summarily avoided from an independent branch of the United States government, left alone to financially survive from the increasing population and services it provides. It was in the early seventies when a first-class stamp cost five cents. Since the beginning of this year, the fifty-cent stamps have gone up to fifty-five cents. This expensive manner to settle monthly bills has been a no-brainer. Coupled with hoarding few Forever stamps when they were twenty cents each, it gives me the latitude of not going to the post office if I have to mail a card or a letter.

There are many ways of facing up to what one owes, though the problem can be avoided or minimized by not going over one's budget. Last year, it was found from a study that for many to pay for their credit required withdrawing from savings 25.89 percent of the time. People also used credit cards 13.56 percent, borrowed money 4.05 percent, sold belongings 1.74 percent, and negotiated an installment plan with the Internal Revenue Service for taxes owed 3.56 percent. For now, I do even not check my credit score, an offshoot of companies created rating people on their credit worthiness, as I have no use for it except once when some companies used it before installing the utilities in our house.

Sometimes an old tradition of being free and clear from financial indiscretions such as debts that are secure or unsecure can be transposed to the present times, where demands for accountability have changed, where credit is oftentimes considered a convenience and a categorical financial advantage and paying your bills is not an activity destined for a mark in a calendar. I would rather be old-fashioned with what I learned growing up in a small village and from a family that finds virtue in not owing an account to anybody.

I sleep better this way.

Casino Life

It's the new age. And since the turn of the century, *casino*, which was originally Italian, meant to be a villa or a summerhouse for music appreciation and for other civic functions, bring friends for dancing and have a good time, has metamorphosed into what we know today. Not only are these "little" houses that used to accommodate these archaic activities but now are towering glamour of hotel rooms, hosting entertainment events, exhibits, shows, shopping areas, restaurants, and the recently added resort amenities to attract families. But the most important characteristic of its etymology and usage is related to all games of chance, often called gambling, which has become an adopted phenomenon worldwide where casinos are found. And they are found almost anywhere, in cities and metropolis where the privilege of having and running a casino is highly sought and extremely competitive, and in areas considered to be *reservations* of natives, whose tribes and status are recognized and exempted from the rigors of paperwork required by the government.

It is not the glitz that pulled me from a sedate but comfortable West Texas town to the periphery of four miles of bright lights called the Strip, the north end of which is Sahara Avenue and the south end, Russell Avenue. It is because of some other reasons, primarily the economics of it all in a city closer to the country across the ocean where I was originally from, where some of my friends in the East Coast moved in their retirement years to escape the harsh winter of discontent they have long endured in their preceding lives. And to be seriously honest, I moved to this state that did not ask me to pony up with state tax, similar to where I lived for thirty-eight years before that. I just hope this would not be altered in the time I intend to stay here. Having established residence in an adjacent locale to this mecca has made all the sights and sounds passé after the initial fervor of seeing and experiencing them. Tourists that interminably come and go during all seasons of the year never tire though, plowing the strip and watching the dancing fountains of the Bellagio. I thought I had seen it all, much like the Statue of Liberty with her right arm stretched holding the vaunted light (I went to the hallowed strip of land in the New York Harbor once) that I saw every day when I took the BQE to the East River Parkway to the hospital on 96th Street many years ago, living in Brooklyn. I did not go to or visit the statue until my family showed the sights of Manhattan to someone from out of town who expressed the desire to see the lady. You see, I am always that way.

Until my friend Arthur mentioned the Mob Museum located in downtown, I did not know that of course, there were much more that I had not been interested in knowing about the place I relocated almost five years ago. I found the three-story place, a restored courthouse and post office building nestled in a corner of Stewart Avenue, a rejuvenating part of a downtown a stone's throw away from Freemont Street, the first paved street in Las Vegas. The city I closely moved to was a dusty town founded, inhabited, and dominated by the mafia who survived over the spilled blood of their rivals. Mobsters like the Jewish gangster Bugsy Siegel, a trusted aide of Charles "Lucky" Luciano and money man Meyer Lansky were crime lords of a vintage city, now transformed several decades later into what is known as the entertainment capital of the world. The city does not claim to be the first of its kind to achieve the title despite the concentration of casinos of the more than a thousand in the country, but it does house some of the richest barons of the gaming industry anywhere in the world. The explosion in the number of casinos built and developed worldwide is growing steadily, an addition to those already in different parts of the globe, the two largest in size being in China and the other in the state called Connecticut. In the country, the largest in total gaming footage until recently is in a small town called Thackerville, Oklahoma. By the way, I went to see the National Museum of Organized Crime and Law Enforcement, part of the determined effort to learn about the history of the now burgeoning city.

If one enters the portals of these gaming houses, the most encountered devices for anyone to drop whatever fortune they have in their pockets would be the slots. That is because the chances of capital appreciation before anyone sits down is a measly 10–12 percent, the rest of the 100 percent total belongs to the house. For the habitués of the place, mostly the crowd with oxygen cannulas attached to and dripping from their noses, from the millennial who unknowingly knows the odds from the blackjack, where the chances are supposedly the best for the bettor than the dealer, or those that consider themselves sophisticated in the ways of plunking their 401Ks, the lure is further advanced by the skimpily clad women who go around enticing customers with free cocktails. My brother Rolly suspected this as one reason why every day that one turns on the TV, the lead news would be a vehicular crash caused by someone incoherent because of taking advantage of these casino inducements.

Not too long ago, there was an article in the *Las Vegas Sun* by Thomas Moore that detailed the revenues of the Strip hitting record levels in 2017 after "seven consecutive losses," a far cry from the state's woes during the recession years. This was because of the non-gaming spending by tourists on such things as food and drinks, other attractions like the resort amenities that have been added to the hotel and gaming activities, attracting more family-oriented tourists in the process. The next year is expected further increase the resort revenues with the parking fees imposed on everyone else who utilizes the casino's parking lots on the Strip.

Mention Las Vegas, and it conjures a place of incessant activity profuse with noise, corruptible fun and events, the savory and unsavory business practices and attractions that proliferate in both the lights and the shadows of an aphrodisiac stage. But shortly after living here in an adjacent town a few minutes away from the boundary of this cosmopolitan city, I found out that it is as quiet as the small town in the West Texas Panhandle I moved from, staying away from the unadulterated atmosphere of Sin City. Of course, we are occasionally drawn to what are called station casinos five to ten minutes away from our gated community, being considered locals, only to keep our membership cards active, to get our loot of Merlot and Cabernet and all varieties of alcohol, which we give away, and our made-in-China gifts that are almost given regularly and while in our house, our visitors are directed to go to the room where we store them if they want to go shopping.

Plus, the parking for us is free.

> *We cannot change the cards we are dealt with. Just how we play the hand.*
>
> *—from the last lecture of Randy Pausch, American professor of computer science, died from pancreatic cancer at age forty-seven*

Eulogy

One of the social obligations that I fulfill every now and then is to go and attend a memorial service for a friend or relative who just passed way. It is more of a duty than an obligation really, and I hope that it does not happen frequently, as I never want to have a friend or relative a subject of an elegy or eulogy. We all know that we will eventually end where we begin—from nothing—some by the unexpected events that we never thought was coming. Some by a lingering illness that we know ends in the panegyric testimonial in an encomium we willfully attend. Whether the friendship was short-lived or long-lasting, the homage and the testimonials usually fall between the zones of memorable events and the platitudes of a life rehashed by those delivering the eulogies at the memorial service, and not necessarily to idealize his or her life. While it is true that there have been some organizations and churches that do not encourage or favor eulogy as a part of the necrological services, it is more common for many to go with the ritual whose use was first documented in the fifteenth century. Fred Phelps, the pastor of the seventy-member, small Westboro Baptist Church in Topeka, Kansas, disbarred as a lawyer in 1979, organized an anti-gay funeral demonstration against Matthew Shepard during the latter's funeral service. This has metamorphosed into protests against funeral corteges and internments of soldiers who died in the Iraq or Afghanistan campaigns and Fred Phelps' vow to continue his congregation's activities to this day, although there is much less fanfare from news media coverage the last few years. The group has reportedly picketed in all fifty states despite the legal obstacles it faced but supported by the Supreme Court's March 2, 2011, ruling on Phelps' First Amendment rights. His antics were nevertheless condemned by Baptist alliances and seminaries. Catholic priests are known to be forbidden at mass to deliver a eulogy in lieu of a homily, a rubric of a rite that has its origin at the Council of Trent in 1545. In all the years I have attended the services of the Church, this edict remains unbroken to my knowledge.

There were two occasions I have been asked to deliver a eulogy, both involving family members. In 1998, I stood up at a church lectern in a crowd of family members and friends to say few words about my mother. It was easy to say my recollections of the things she liked and disliked, of growing up knowing that among the children I was obviously her favorite, although when asked who was closest to her chest, she always said that the thirteen she raised were all treated the same. My six brothers and six sisters later figured out otherwise. It was also poignant because of the way she carried herself from the disease process that lasted for a few years—up to this day, how and where in her constitution and DNA contracted the illness that she and her family had to deal with full support and with grace. I did not think then that I would last the few minutes I summarized what I knew of her without tearing up. But delivering a homage for your mother brings in you a resolute determination to isolate yourself from being a subjective son to an objective discloser of a life well-lived.

In 2014, a day before Christmas, my father-in-law passed way at 103 and 1/2 years old. It necessitated and adjustment to our scheduled departure for a surgical mission we annually were involved in, to attend his services in the Philippines, where he was known in military, medical, and prominent alumni circles, he being a pediatrician, a retired colonel in the army, and among the longest survivors of the Death March. My father died when he was only 59, and for the next four decades and some, my father-in-law became a surrogate as a father figure who adored my children and all his grandchildren from his wife who passed away 9 years before him. I was asked to say a few words during his wake, which I dutifully did, stammering events of the happy association my family had with him and the kinship we developed over the years. I have not been asked to share my thoughts and experiences at a memorial service of a relative or a friend since and hope that it would be the last I will be asked to.

One of the hardest responsibilities of a man of the cloth is when he or she is asked to preside over the memorial service of someone whose relatives claim that the deceased was a member of his church. He is certain that he doesn't know the individual, who was not a regular churchgoer, to say the least, and never contributed to the activities, both financial and social, of the church. But as expected of a minister of a church chosen by the local elders, he acquiesces with the demands, contacts the family members about short biography and anything good that he can say about the individual during the necrological services. In a situation like this, anything that is said about the good and possibly the bad and the ugly about the decedent is not heartfelt but simply an empty panegyric to fulfill the wishes of the living distant and not-so-distant relatives. Things would have been better if those who advocate for a decedent did not suddenly become so religious to have their dead family relative have the trappings of a service most churches can't say no to. It would even be better if the individual declares before he is dead about how he should be disposed of. Like Jeffrey Dahmer, who never wanted public funeral and had his beaten body cremated. Or Ted Bundy, who was eventually caught, executed, and his ashes spread over the Cascade Mountains, where four of his thirty-plus victims were found. And John Wayne Gacy, the amiable serial killer whose four-year crime spree of more than forty victims caught up with him and landed him in prison, never was given the memorial service and eulogy after his execution.

According to its definition, a eulogy is a commendatory oration in honor of a recently deceased friend or relative and the positive impacts his or her life had on the family, friends, and the community. It is such an emotionally overwhelming task for anyone delivering it that I personally do not want any of my friends or relatives, when my time comes, to be subjected to these terms of endearment.

A short prayer will do.

Friendship and Friends

No. It is not *Friends*, the television sitcom that ran for ten years and the reruns still shown daily on TV has made those that starred in the series rich from the residuals they continue to receive. It is not about the ensemble of three men and three women in Manhattan who always come up with their own raconteurs for every situation there is in their lairs and their lives. While obviously there exists some form of friendship among them, what with chaos created in almost every situation they are in, it is more of the type of utilitarian friendship Aristotle described in his treatise "The Nichomachean Ethics." Aristotle describes this friendship as "shallow," easily dissolved, and is brought to the relationship by another person. I have watched many episodes of this sitcom, which I find sometimes interesting, with some of the characters' tantrums fracturing their relationships and friendships, only to be repaired on the next episode.

Friendship and having friends are an integral part of being what we are. We start developing the habit during our childhood when we play and learn together, when we care and share in things that we do. While friendship and friends can change and later grow apart, the shared common experiences are harder to part with even if friendship is developed "passing through" in life, as C. C. Ryder once sang in his 1974 ditty. Mostly, according to Aristotle, this type of friendship, motivated by pleasure, is only accidental and short-lived and apt to change over time. I do not argue with his assertions that this type of friendship is between people who are witty, based on good looks, young and passionate and looking for something that is pleasant to one's core. Looking at what characteristics I possess from the start tells me I can never belong to the second type of friends and friendship he described in his Nichomachean Ethics.

But I believe that true friendship is a virtue especially if it is based on respect, honesty, and trust. True that there is no friendship that exists among crooks, but when true friends form perfect friendship, it is based on goodness, where one strives for the goodness of the other. Some people make sacrifices to the extent of giving up their lives for a friend. No one exemplifies this trait that Jesus Christ himself, who, on the day that he was to be arrested, exhorted his disciples, in John 15:13, to "Love one another. No one has greater love than this to lay down one's life for one's friend." Which brings me to Paul Wesley or Ronald Shurer and the other Medal of Honor recipients. The philosopher Euripides said, "Friends show their love in times of trouble, not in times of happiness." I do not know them personally, but knowing that they were willing to give up their lives for the sake of their friends and comrades, I wanted to count them as true friends, which is what Joe was to me.

Although he was not as heroic as the Medal of Honor recipients, I still think that he was a true friend. We started our friendship in grade school; it culminated in college and got through adulthood when we went on in different directions in life. But Joe was a good listener, was loyal and trustful, and the things we talked about remained between us. I chanced upon him one day when we were having an alumni reunion. It had been many years, and both of us had gray hairs on our pate, indicative of how many years it has been since we were friends. To this day, I would not hesitate to confide the info I dare not have any other person know about me. I am confident that even at this stage in our lives, Joe wouldn't talk behind my back.

In a recent poll conducted to know how many friends an average person has in a lifetime, it was found that majority had nine "close friends" (and this did not include relatives), 45 percent said they had six or more, 39 percent had between three and five, and 14 percent had one or two close ones. I am not sure about what dynamics of being a close friend the poll used, but if it consisted of certain personal characteristics such as being compassionate, always loyal and trustworthy, and supportive at all times, then I would say that I have more than enough that I could call my friends.

Most people measure how well society treats you and how much material possessions you have amassed in a lifetime. I have always declined to be measured by the latter but the other parameters such as the number of friends I have. Better a few, though, who are considered virtuous, good, and true friends than the many who think that friendship is only for their own sake.

> *True friends are the ones who never leave your heart, even if they leave your life for a while. Even after years apart, you pick up with them right where you left off, and even if they die, they're never dead in your heart.*
>
> *Unknown*
>
> *Friends are much better tried in bad fortune than in good.*
>
> *Aristotle*

Genealogy

Time magazine a few years ago had a picture of an American woman on its cover. It was an amalgamation of phenotype diversity the country was experiencing at that time, where the analysis of the population and the composition of the country's future appeared to be influenced by immigration and interracial marriages resulting in a mixed ancestry. The underlying projections were that the percentage of white immigrants—those that came from Southern and Eastern Europe who comprised the majority of the present American population—will decline in the year 2050 and that the immigrants from Asia and Latin America, especially those from the latter, will change the racial and ethnic composition of the US population. This change will have societal and political implications, the thesis continues, with these groups trying to integrate in the prevailing American society while maintaining the culture and identity of where they came from and the heritage that comes with it. We see it in the past and more so now as the political structure of government is a mixture of racial and mixed-ethnic representation. Thus, we now see that the levers of government diverse as the attitudes and the assumptions of the current population, which is increasingly multicultural and complex especially for the recent settlers in the United States. The Hispanic and Latino people now comprise 18 percent of the 327 million total US population according to the recent US Census, African-Americans amounting to 12.7 percent, while the other 5.6 percent from the other geographical areas of the world constitute the remainder of the non-Hispanic nonwhites as Asian-Americans such as Chinese, Filipinos, or Indians. Sixty-four percent Caucasians and their descendants still constitute the present majority of the population, which, as conflicting projections predict, will eventually be superseded by a mixed breed of Americans in the years to come. It has always been a closely held truism that a country is enriched by immigrants that eventually settled and formed a nation. America was from the outset a multiethnic and multicultural society, from the early settlers in the seventeenth and eighteenth centuries from Europe, and the indentured peoples from Africa and the Caribbean, and the subsequent displacement and absorption of the indigenous peoples of the discovered continent of North America. But things have moved to the present and while the differing ideologies and identities exist in a fluid society such as the United States, changes in a society that is in constant flux are never fixed or immutable.

I was reminded a few weeks ago about this aspect of racial difference and diversity we are born with, while surfing and finally settling on watching one of the beauty pageants on television. Of the more than a dozen beauty contests held every year, the Miss Universe Beauty Pageant was holding its sixty-seventh competition at the Impact Arena in Bangkok, Thailand. Of the ninety-four contestants, all in their twenties, except for a few who were ethnically noticeable as representatives of their country, the rest all looked phenotypically similar, their demographic origins and where they live indicative of the blur immigration, interracial marriage and ancestry bring. Consider the subsequent winner of the pageant, Catriona Gray, who is an Australian citizen born in Cairn, Australia, to a Scottish father and a Filipina mother, graduated from a Boston college, representing the Philippines and not looking like a typical Filipina. Or Miss Nepal, Manita Devkota, who does not look Nepalese, graduated from a North Carolina university and presently established her domicile in North Carolina. Despite the supercontinent that existed during the Pangaea age and the expectation that population would all look alike therefore, the shift of land mass occurring in stages 350 million years ago resulted in the formation of present-day oceans and continents and countries with different climates, environment structures, and habitats. More important is the typical appearance of the inhabitants of the countries created by these tectonic shifts. Thus, Africans, Chinese, Arabs, Europeans, Asians, etc. look different. While it seems that every one of the contestants tries to be monolithic in appearance and not of the country they represent except for the traditional costume they wear and parade in one segment of the competition, it is made up of the female gender only and a small slice of a society and does not identify with the many that may alter the makeup of the population of a country where they want to immigrate, be assimilated, and be a part of. I predict that this contest of how we value the pulchritude of women will invariably be altered from now on by the first transgender contestant, Angela Ponce, promulgated by the country of Spain, where she comes from.

Two years ago while attending a wedding to my sister's daughter in Tennessee (my sister is married to an Irish-American), my son, who is himself married to my blonde, blue-eyed daughter-in-law, brought test tubes for me and my wife to individually fill up to determine our ancestry composition, maternal and paternal haplogroups, health risks and traits, our ethnic origin, from a genetic testing company recently formed, a beneficiary of Watson-Crick DNA discovery. It was no surprise that the results came back and one of them showed that I was almost 100 percent of Asian/Malayan descent and a smattering of a few racial genes that, judging from my looks and the color of my skin, grossly tell me and anyone else about my heritage and where I originally came from. In fact, people will recognize me as coming from a different race in the country of which I now have called myself a citizen for half a century. I cannot argue with what the molecule shaped like a twisted ladder that James Watson and Francis Crick discovered in 1953 (for which they, together with Rosalind Franklin and Maurice Wilkins, received the Nobel Prize in physiology in 1962) tells me how my genes came about and how it plays a role in the processes that brought me my son and my daughter. The double helix of nucleotides and the subsequent discoveries of its extensions have contributed to forensic science and the appearance of the future American on the cover of *Time* magazine. Surprisingly, my wife has more ancestry origins in her blood than she could imagine. That she had progenitors that were Jewish or Chinese was a shock to us all, but looking back, there were many of these racial and ethnic groups that in the past and presently were integrated in the society and country where we all came from.

Every time I power the television on, an item detailing the continued saga of people wanting to move to a different landscape for better opportunities that exist somewhere else than where they originally are from or to escape the prevailing and precarious conditions they find themselves in. In effect, if they are successful, they would alter and ultimately change the face of the country they move to. The composition of the population would change.

Having lived here for most of my adult life, I have contributed to this change in the demographics of the country. My children, grandchildren, nephews and nieces, and relatives have become nondescript faces of the future generations of Americans that eventually make up hopefully the cover of a magazine. Meanwhile, I will not wait to change the way I look, even though I have been assimilated in a society of Asian-Americans that constitute a small percentage of the US population, to which I presently belong.

Even if I wait, it won't happen because I won't be around for a million years.

> *Genealogy itself is something of a privilege, coming far more easily to those of us for whom enslavement, conquest, and dispossession of our land has not been our lot.*
>
> —Tim Wise, American Anti-racial activist and writer
>
> *Genealogy: a perverse preoccupation of those who seek to demonstrate that their forebears were better people than they are.*
>
> Sydney J. Harris Canadian Judge, lawyer and activist

Going to Church

On most weekends, you will find me attending services and listening to the homily of the reverend pastor of the church I belong to. It is an obligation that I have been doing since I could even make the sign of the cross that identifies me as a Christian. The holy days and all the dogma the church has prescribed its followers for centuries have always been commandments that believers of a faith practice at varying degrees in their lives. Faith as I know it is not visible or can't be explained but complete trust in a set of facts for which intellectual assent is a necessity. I learned this concept many years ago from the three grandmothers that raised me much as they did my father early on, all of them spinsters, so religious that every day at four o'clock in the morning, they woke up, kneeling before several portraits and figures of saints illuminated by flickering candles to say their novenas or their prayers. I was many times forced to participate in their veneration but never was asked to join mandatorily in their daily ritual. I just hope that heaven, if it does exist as they believe it does, is accommodating as an eternal destiny for the many years they walked the face of this earth.

Man, despite his conquest and his many attempts to be a supreme being, has always invoked that someone superior to him exists that he can lean on to or ask for wisdom, especially when he engages in activities to advance his powers. This practice is why many religions today such as Hinduism have as many as 320,000,000 gods and goddesses worshipped for every human endeavor. To the extent that idolatry devoted to nonhumans as was in ancient times, paganism is seldom practiced today. There are roughly about 4,200 religions with their churches, temples, and places of worship in the world. I belong, as does my family, to one of the three monotheistic Abrahamic faiths, to be called a Christian, the other two being Judaism and Islam. If Pew Research were to be believed, in the year 2050, the Christian population and its different denominations would exceed 3.0 billion, although Islam would overtake Christianity by 2070. The Catholic Church is the largest Christian church with 1.3 billion baptized in survey conducted in 2016.

There are many facets to every religion or church that one belongs to. For example, Buddhism, or Hinduism as it is in Japan, Thailand, or India, does not evangelize or proselytize to other peoples to increase the number of their followers. One is born into or adopts the faith, as one believes it is a way to nirvana or to salvation. On the other hand, the Abrahamic religion comprised of the three monotheistic denominations has been divisive since the apocryphal inception of Judaism and Christianity. Each, together with Eastern Orthodox Christianity, starting in the first century, have tried to exert the superiority and dominance of their beliefs, although each one worships one and same or similar God in their doctrine. Religious wars and different campaigns were prevalent, such as the Crusades initiated and sanctioned by Pope Urban in 1095, with the Islamic and Christian cultures clashing for many centuries. Sadly, the conflicts between these religions continue up to the present with clearly demarcated differences noticeably in the Middle East. Splinter groups among similar religions such as Islam's Shiite and Sunni, Orthodox and non-Orthodox Jews and multiple denominations sprouting from Martin Luther's Reformation involving the Christian faith although the latter do not seem to be characterized by vitriol or violence.

Many years ago, for the second time in my lifetime, I visited as part of a tour of the Holy Land the ancient places mentioned in the old scrolls, Jerusalem being the confluence of the three major religions that is known today. It is confounding and hard to imagine that in a land and a city that spawned the major disciples and characters responsible for the Torah, the Bible, and the Quran, people can't find peace even in the twenty-first century. The Dome of the Rock and Al-Aqsa Mosque, the Via Dolorosa, and the Temple Mount, which is shared between all three, stand as testament to the traditions and the significance of the religions that Abraham was said to be the origin. The Wailing Wall, Western Wall, Kotel, or as Islam calls it, Buraq Wall and its connection to the Temple Mount was not lost as a destination. This limestone edifice built by Herod in 19 BCE, visited by millions of tourists every year, was a holy place where on a piece of paper was written the few supplications that I inserted into one of its crevices. I still am waiting to this day the answers to my prayers.

There have been 266 popes through the founding of the Catholic Church. During its continuous existence, the papacy has been racked by dissension, ascension, controversy, conspiracy, and charges of nepotism, sometimes murders to gain and perpetuate its hold not only of spiritual but temporal powers. The modern papacy however has re-established itself as a spiritual force to the world and to majority of its adherents, including myself who at times question the authority of those who clothe themselves in a holy frock that hides the opulence and corpulence on a proscribed holy day. It is a question I ask: why Islam or the Muslims who venerate the prophet Muhammad as a messenger of Allah violate the precepts of peace and love enunciated by the Quran and Judaism separates itself into the non-Orthodox and Orthodox segments of its faith. Does anyone wonder that if those that are involved in commercial ventures pay royalties to the saints and the Messiah for whom they use their names or likenesses in the wares they sell to the public? It is one of the reasons why I am so uncomfortable with those who profit from establishing themselves a disciple of a particular faith by creating and naming a church they call their own. Or kneeling and praying in an ornate church or cathedral in places I have seen particularly in an effort to attract members or acolytes of the faith.

The way to heaven, according to all or many religions, is as many there are roads that lead to this eternal place. I am a Christian, a Catholic and probably won't change to another from the religion I was born in or have faith in despite the many faults I find it harbored in the past and in the present. I would rather worship in a small and nondescript church and wake up at four o'clock in the morning like my late grandmothers kneeling in veneration to the saints with the lights of flickering candles.

> *A religion that gives nothing, costs nothing, and suffers nothing, is worth nothing.*
>
> *Martin Luther, a priest who led the Protestant Reformation*
>
> *If you have two religions in your land, the two will cut each other's throat; but if you have thirty religions, they dwell in peace.*
>
> *Voltaire (nom de plume of Francoise-Marie Arouet), French historian and philosopher*

Reunions

Ever had any of these reunions, family, class, groups, or any that people in charge of organizing these periodic get-togethers think of? I have been to all of them, mind you. It seems there is one around the corner every time I turn my head around, which, more often than not, I do.

In 1990, I had my first family reunion. As our family was scattered across the country (I found out that this was the prevalent aggrupation), we decided to hold it in a neutral zone, in Myrtle Beach, South Carolina. Thirteen of us, seven brothers and six sisters, made the arrangements over the phone. It was so exciting to plan for this first-time event in our life, something that we had heard about but never had the resources to carry out. You see, it was not because of having put it in the very back of our minds, but going through the daily stress of growing up in a poor family environment that became a centerpiece of our daily existence. But now in a different land, married with most of us gainfully employed and with growing children of our own, we decided to have it. We could afford it, if only for once in our lifetime. We rented three adjacent houses, rooms were apportioned to the numbers in each family, and meals to every kitchen and dining table were rotated.

My widowed mother and my visiting father-in law were the prime additions to the thirteen of us and the twenty-eight grandchildren, the birthdays of each my mother remembered and recited in a heartbeat. I still wonder up to now how she did it without the memory enhancement pills that now abound. Prevagen did not exist then; organic brain syndrome, which we know nowadays as Alzheimer's, was the prevailing term in the medical lexicon. The three-day affair was full of planned activities, sitting for pictures and photographs that involved the whole family, with my mother always occupying the hallowed center, a few jokes and speeches and reminiscing on the past. My eight-year-old son caught a small shark the size of my forearm from fishing along the shores of Atlantic Ocean. It did not survive the hook that got him into the unwanted captivity. At the conclusion of the reunion, the family was brought closer together.

The activity extended in some form. I heard that my sisters on the East Coast, who all live nearby, meet every Friday in the afternoon at someone else's house over a cup of coffee and doughnuts, exchanging pleasantries and weekly gossip. In the middle of the Southwest, where we live, and some of my brothers in the West Coast, because of the distance, precluded us from joining them in this weekly ritual.

In June of 2015, my niece Kate, the daughter of my sister Tita and her husband Jimmy, an Irish-American, decided that we would have another reunion. The children we had in 1990 were all grown up now, some of them were married, others in a relationship. Most of us have become grandparents. Funny that some still had very dark and abundant hair while some have silver and white thinning manes. For as long as we did not go through the hassles of organizing and the younger ones took the helm, we agreed to have it. It was held again at Myrtle Beach, South Carolina, and despite the idea of returning to where we billeted ourselves a quarter of century ago, things had changed with the times. We could not identify where we stayed before and have to stay at different and adjacent hotels. Except for my twelve siblings and their spouses and their children (Jim and my mother passed away years back), there were over a hundred this time. Compared to forty-three the first time, you could see why it was hard to remember all the names of the new participants and the significant others my now-older nephews and nieces brought along to this family event. I supposed they consider them already members of the burgeoning family base. But the brothers and sisters plus their spouses were just as accommodating, especially that we were spared from shouldering their temporary upkeep.

Class reunions are a different breed. My class of 1970 (half of whom are here and the other half saw to it that they remain for postgraduate training at home rather than go abroad) gathers every so often, maybe every five years, to see how everyone is doing. The first few times this happened give you the feeling that no one would like to break away from the close relationships developed during college years. There was no need to slap on the left side of your chest your name on a piece of paper, identifying who you are just in case memory fades and you do not know who copied surreptitiously from you during one of those exams.

Grand reunion occurs after you have lasted for twenty-five years, during which time you are obligated to tell somebody who has the temerity to ask what pills you have to take and how many heart attacks you have suffered since the last reunion, no longer the number of children you have nor what you have been doing during earlier times. Now this happens every year, though I have stopped attending these grand reunions, as people who find these organized gatherings and activities have become predictable. Like me, I no longer get choked over a story told and repeated so many times during these class encounters. What brings me to sad ennui is the list of classmates who in an earlier part of these proceedings have departed a promising life.

Many times, I am reminded of Dr. Mahlon Ingham, one of the old practitioners in the West Texas town where I eventually settled for thirty-eight years. He was an Okie, graduated from Oklahoma University, crusty, capable, but gentle. He always ribbed me that he came from a school of hard knocks, that he survived and had a flourishing practice in this panhandle town. Every five years, he always made it a point to attend his class reunion in Oklahoma. When he returned from these events despite the joys recalling the past, there were two reports that he always said: the members of his class who were incapacitated by physical illnesses—the result of advancing years—and the names of his classmates who did not make it because of deaths. He and the remaining members of his class suggested that they make their reunion every year hence, and that day they did. He did not make it the following year, because shortly thereafter, he himself had a fatal heart attack.

I attended his funeral service. I could still feel the hair on my neck rising when during his memorial service, he sang in his own taped CD and deep basso profundo voice a hymn I often heard him hum before he scrubbed going to the operating room.

I am again attending some of these reunions. And while they are a way of recalling the past, they are also a reminder of what is ahead in of us in the future.

> *When we recall the past, we usually find that it is the simplest things, not the great occasions, that in retrospect give off the greatest glow of happiness.*
>
> —Bob Hope, American actor and comedian

Code Blue Above the Clouds

It is seldom that you hear the overhead speaker in a plane that asks for a medical doctor or personnel on board to please proceed and contact the nearest flight attendant. You will know then that there must be an in-flight emergency aboard that requires immediate attention and response. It is also very infrequent, sometimes not at all, that the emergencies are known unless you personally hear about them. Majority are underreported, and what happens to the patient-passengers after they leave the plane is not known. In the United States, airlines are required by the Federal Aviation Administration to report only those events where a passenger dies or if a plane is diverted because of death or medical emergency. It is one reason why in-flight medical events do not make the news.

    I listened to a doctor friend of mine's account of his experience with some modicum of interest, knowing that such occurrences are rare—one for every 10,000 to 40,000 passengers in intercontinental flights. So flying from Madrid to Dallas-Fort Worth last May, 30,000 feet above the Atlantic Ocean, was just another flight, coming from a three-week sojourn in Portugal and Spain. Then it happened, when through the plane's PA system came the urgent page about a medical doctor on board needed for someone in the back cabin being in shock. There were four of us who responded, a couple who were doctors, aided by two female nurses who also came to respond to the emergency. The passenger-patient was a nun who was noted to be a diabetic and a hypertensive and, after appropriate resuscitation using the plane's medical kit, got off eventually at DFW airport when the plane landed and was whisked off to a nearby medical facility.

While a standardized recording of in-flight medical emergency is sadly lacking, there is a growing body of studies that onboard emergencies are on the rise. Melissa Mattison and Mark Zeidel in a paper published in *JAMA* in 2011 cited a survey by European airlines that revealed 10,000 medical emergency events over a five-year period. Americans are traveling and flying more than ever. US airlines alone transported 732 million passengers in 2012. It is projected that this will reach a billion in 2024. Worldwide, more than a billion people travel by air each year, and more seniors and older people are traveling as well, a trend that is on the rise. Older people have more medical problems and therefore carry higher risks of having in-flight emergencies, especially if they ignore or neglect to ensure their fitness for air travel.

There were a number of surveys and reports that give information about which medical problems are most common. According to health and policy professor Richard Stefanici's 2012 paper published in *Clinical Geriatrics*, the biggest cause of in-flight deaths are cardiac issues, notably heart attack. The most common onboard emergencies include temporary loss of consciousness or fainting, hyperventilation, shortness of breath and chest pain, complications due to diabetes and gastrointestinal issues. Life-threatening deep vein thrombosis also occurs especially among older travelers, although only about 200 cases were reported during a ten-year period between 1993 and 2003.

We carry heavy luggage between gates and terminals, which are generally far apart. We cross different time zones, resulting in a complicated medication schedule. Some of us travel to relax, leave our worries behind, and consequently drink alcohol or take relaxants. Some have this fear of flying or are anxious, which makes them stressed and exacerbates whatever they are suffering from. Because of cramped quarters and a 10 percent drop in blood oxygen saturation among air travelers because the cabin is pressurized to the equivalent of 5,000 to 8,000 feet above sea level, flying is dauntingly harsh especially for people with chronic illnesses or pre-existing medical conditions. In many instances, these passengers board the aircraft without consulting their doctors, who probably would have recommended that they not fly. When they do go and have an in-flight medical emergency that can only be resolved by diverting the plane to an unscheduled destination, the decision to divert the flight is an expensive proposition, with additional landing fees, missed connections for other passengers, and at times causing pilots and the crew to cancel their FAA-sanctioned duty day limits. An emergency landing of a domestic flight can cost about $30,000, that of an international flight $70,000 to $230,000.

Physicians and other medical personnel responding to in-flight medical emergencies are protected under the "good Samaritan" provision of the Air Carrier Access Act of 1998. Under this legislation, "an individual shall not be liable for damages in any action brought in a Federal or State courts arising out of acts or omissions of the individual in providing or attempting to provide assistance in the case of in-flight emergency unless the individual while rendering such assistance is guilty of gross negligence or willful misconduct." There have not been any documented cases of physicians being sued who provided assistance during an emergency in-flight event.

The challenges a responding physicians faces are tough and include such things as cramped quarters with space limited to treat the passenger, the onboard emergency kit not readily available, the unfamiliarity of the layout and the contents of the emergency kit, and at times, the unavailability of flight attendants to help. For physicians to respond to such an emergency, some advice given by Drs. Chandra and Condy of the American College of Emergency Physicians include (1) Introduce yourself to the cabin crew and state your qualifications. (2) Ask if a patient can respond, for his permission while performing a thorough history and physical examination. (3) Use an interpreter if necessary. (4) If the patient's condition is critical, request a diversion to the nearest airport. (5) Cooperate with the medical response center and coordinate with the airport medical staff. (6) Keep a written record of your patient encounter. (7) Perform only treatments you are qualified to administer.

The chances of having a doctor on the plane are surprisingly good. In a 1991 FAA study, physicians were available in 85 percent of the recorded emergencies. These days, it is even better since flights are often booked to capacity. However, there are times when no medical or health professional is on board to respond or help during in-flight medical emergencies. If this happens, every airline provides flight crews access to medical staff advice during these emergencies. Many airlines now use the services of remote emergency response centers such as MedAire's Medlink Global Response Center which provides worldwide real-time assistance twenty-four hours a day, seven days a week. Flight attendants can talk to Medlink ground doctors, who can direct appropriately what actions to take. In 2011, MedAire handled 22,000 in-flight medical emergency calls.

There are no federal regulations or guidelines in the management of in-flight medical emergencies. However, the Federal Aviation Administration requires all US commercial airlines weighing 7,500 pounds or more and serviced by one or more flight attendant to carry a defibrillator and enhanced medical emergency kit and be certified in CPR including the use of AED every two years. The pilots are also required to know how to use the AED. While the medical kit does not have what is generally in a hospital crash cart, the transport medical committee of the American Medical Association recommends that a standard medical kit must include a stethoscope, syringes and IV catheters of several sizes, and the commonly used medications such as atropine, epinephrine 1:1,000, dextrose 50 percent, nitroglycerine, anticonvulsants, diuretic, normal saline, bronchial dilator inhaler, and others. Most domestic airlines carry this kit. There are, however, no international regulations that require a complete kit to be available.

Nobody wants to get sick on an airplane. While the airline industry develops a standardized protocol to help survive in-flight medical emergencies, the best approach is avoiding it in the first place. For older travelers and for those with medical conditions that can be adversely affected by air travel, a pre-flight evaluation by a physician or health care provider is recommended. Similarly, the physician should be responsible enough to tell their patients whether they should travel or not and if they could, what steps they need to do to prevent the event from happening. It is then that we don't have to expect the unexpected.

> *There are only two reasons to sit in the back row of an airplane: Either you have diarrhea, or you're anxious to meet people who do.*
>
> *—Henry Kissinger, former Secretary of State*
>
> *Airplane travel is nature's way of making you look like your passport photo.*
>
> *—Al Gore, former senator from Tennessee and vice president of the United States*

What's in a Name?

Anyone born in a country that was under Spain for more than three centuries inevitably will have his or her parents give him or her a Castilian or Latin American name. It is a custom that changed a pagan or early Malay prefix to attach to one's native suffix. Something like the name Luis, Jose, or Fernando if it were a man, and Luisa or Maria or Constancia if it were a woman—all were too common then. Except for the southern part of the country, where the Muslims and Islamic religion were domiciled in the country found by Magellan in 1521, this practice persisted, promulgated at baptisms by missionary priests who had almost the power of selecting the names—recommendations, as they called it—every time an infant was brought to the font, where 85 percent are known to be Christians. While this tradition gradually changed at the turn of the century, when the Americans came and stayed for slightly more than fifty years following Admiral Dewey's defeat of the Spanish Armada at Manila Bay, the practice of naming names following the Spanish way continued. Thus, my brothers were named after the parish priests in my hometown—Arcadio, Jaime, Fred, Ignacio, Rolando, Pedro. My sisters were named Teresita, Susanna, Esther, etc. I was surprised later to find that my name was Edward—that among family members and the rest of my classmates in school, I had a name that was different. I learned later on that when my father approached his cousin to stand as my godmother during my baptism, she would only do it on one condition—that my name was to be the name of her American husband or else she would not acquiesce to being supportive of the supplication. To this day, I'm not even sure why my godmother Nena married her husband, whom I did not have the pleasure of meeting as he succumbed to the excesses apparently of alcohol. Her sons, by the way, were named with Anglo Caucasians' appellations.

My father readily agreed to her demand, and I was officially called by my godmother's husband's name. But in a meek deal with my dad, she did not oppose the idea of inserting as my middle name the given name of my paternal grandfather. I did not use this name whenever I was asked to write my middle name or initial; rather, I used my mother's maiden family name instead, as was and is still customary. Besides, while it is a middle name, it was the name of a very well-known and famous Spanish philosopher with whom I sometimes wanted to be mistakenly associated. I do use my paternal grandfather's name occasionally when asked for a password for some of my devices.

A parent has the privilege of naming his or her child. Whether it is a duty or right, we gave serious thought about a name that is euphonic, that will wear well during childhood and adulthood, and that the child will respond to when called. In my case, it is all of these, but in keeping with the prevailing mood and tradition, it was like the Western or English common law of names. And so, my good wife and I decided on a name for a son that denotes strength over gentility. The second one that came along, our daughter, was named not for the most popular name in the country that year but something simple and common. But it was not Castilian or of Latin origin. Of course, we have given them informal monikers when calling them casually, not totally derived from their formal names but nevertheless terms of endearment. In contravention to his parents' attempt at being in step with the Western crowd in naming their offspring, my son later gave his three daughters Latin and Italian-derived names and call buttons. He found it fashionable and different and pleasing to the ears to impart to each one of them names that he heard when he spent part of his undergraduate studies in Italy and Greece. It is a good thing though, from my perspective, that he did not give them the names of the saints and the pressure of the lives associated with their names—not that I have anything against the saints, because I venerate them. It is only because the coming of the new order and trying to Anglicize names of the saints reminded me of the more than three centuries my country was a colony of Spain.

It is universally accepted nowadays that an individual's personal name includes a given name, a family name or surname despite some variations from country to country. The use of last name is just as recent as the sixteenth century in the West, although it was practiced in China thousands of years BC, when the reigning emperor decreed then than his subjects use inherited family names or surnames. There is also the question of a woman who gets married and assumes the family name of her husband and whether this custom is widespread. Children born out of this union automatically carry the man's family name. There has been a recent move, though it has not been codified into law, that a married woman can retain her own given and family name in her profession, although the majority of married women prefer to assume their husband's surname. A small percentage of men nowadays are reversing the trend; instead, they are assuming the wives' family names and giving up their own surnames especially when the woman they are married to is more prominent economically and socially. A stamp to this reverse sui generis can be sealed in a courthouse.

While we do not have the choice that our parents have when they give us our names, as we become more aware of what we are called by the society we interact with, we either accept without question what we have been christened or, if given the privilege in later life, change our names to our liking without changing who we have become. So my brothers, when they finally became citizens of this country and were given the option of changing their names, came up with the sound that erased the call of Arcadio to the more urbane Richard, Rolando to Roland, Pedro to Peter, Ignacio to Naz, Jaime to Jim, and Fred to Freddie. Their given names became indelible in their licenses or their passports and papers that were part of their identity. Their names finally came to be like mine—Anglo-Saxon from the time I was baptized. Some of my sisters though did not do so because they did not want the hassles of the change in their transcripts, certificates, and documents though I heard that there never was any opposition or conflicts from their spouses.

Akila, Fayth, Makayla, Ahmood, Jamal, Dajon. Ever hear or see these names? I see them on television every time I turn it on, especially if I surfed toward sports or if one of the anchors was of African-American origin. Naming names that identify what race or ethnic background one comes from has become the norm among the younger generation, freed from what was once a sacred order from parents or forebears who conformed to existing mores. Such names as Kuan-Yin or Lin, Lian or Qoun are unmistakably Chinese. And if it is a boy, it connotes strength and prosperity, characteristics that the baby exhibits in adulthood. It does not always follow, though, about the power of names and what is believed by many that names can help you be molded into what you become but not determine who you will be. Whether one is Muslim or Islamic or Jewish, anyone can readily discern the roots of an individual by their names.

I did never change my name. But now I wish I did. From what it is to what I think now, living in an era where my name has become commonplace in the country where I am now, not knowing my identity and appreciating that as a non-Caucasian, I am as creative and resourceful as anyone. I found out that being Fernando, Luis, or Jose Maria (names that were around three hundred years ago during the Spanish conquest of my country and exist to this day) has an aura that remains alluring and romantic. Unlike my brothers, if I were given any of these names, I wouldn't mind at all, like my son who was sagacious enough in naming his daughters Olivia, Noemi, and Isabelle.

> *Tigers die and leave their skins. People die and leave their names.*
>
> *Proverb*

Surrogacy

Moving into a new start from a big metropolis like New York City to a small town in West Texas with a population of about two thousand souls, bringing with me my family consisting of my wife and two small children was a culture shock that each of us never expected in this move. But having lived and survived the hustle of further training in some of the best and biggest medical centers in the country and the grind of daily existence in a city of eight million and an amalgam of different cultures, I was ready to try and settle with a different ambience in the other parts of the country. The house we rented was small enough to accommodate the meager furniture we brought from our seven-year stay in an apartment in the city. Though we did, after a year, move to built or purchased domiciles in different locales in the county, the rented house we initially had was ten minutes away from the small hospital where I was called to attend to critical patients eventually. The traffic was sparse, the roads were so wide that I found driving was a zip compared to the potholed roads and the heavy traffic that was a 24/7 adventure in the jungles of Brooklyn and Manhattan.

  I remember living on a small street where the mayor of the small town had his house. Our two children did not complain about the only day school where they enrolled in town, though most of the lesson plans were repeats of what they studied in the city before the move. The three children of the mayor, who was married to one of the hospital board members' daughter, were just inured to city-slicker extravaganzas but were just contented and happy in the accouterments of a small-town atmosphere. In West Texas and most Southwest rural towns, a neighbor becomes a friend, and the secrets one holds close to the vest ultimately become known to everyone else who proffers to keep them in confidence like their own. It was an iniquity getting used to. The three, the mayor, and his wife and their extended family migrated to us for their medical needs. I suppose that the allure of someone coming from a big medical center in a big city brought the change from using for many years prior to our arrival, the old practitioners schooled in hard knocks and who were as experienced and qualified as us. We liked the small-town atmosphere so much so that we defied the prevailing statistics at that time where a medical provider moved at least five times in his or her professional career. We stayed despite the short interval where the only hospital in town was closed because of the internecine disputes that surfaced between the employees, the board, the administrator, and the medical staff. It even made the national news one day, that many other medical centers offered us amenities to move to their places. But we persevered and stayed for more than just professional reasons. We stayed until John Jr. (the only son of the mayor), who had a luscious head of hair growing up, lost all of it after he got married for the second time. Marie, the eldest daughter, and her younger sister got married eventually. Marie moved to Colorado, had two children of her own, and became the superintendent of a school district. Her children went to a university where they lettered in physical sports. The younger sister, Therese, though appearing like she was in perfect health, had issues that required her going a number of times to undergo heart operations in Houston. Very bright and accomplished, she became as well a principal in her hometown and had many accolades appended to her career that the faces of the former mayor now and his wife lit up whenever they talked about it.

 Which brings me to the subject at hand. Therese was married to a man (also my erstwhile patient) whose parents were divorced but were on my patient list as well; because of her medical condition, pregnancy in her case was ruled out by those taking care of her.

The couple, as I came to know later, did not opt for adoption where, among other things, the mother considering giving up her child can change her mind, whereas in some other states, a pregnant surrogate mother cannot. In the final analysis, they decided for surrogacy. While at the outset, I was not all interested nor keyed up to what the concept was all about, because of the relationship we had developed with the parents and the couple as they grew up to adulthood, I became inquisitive about what the process was, whether and how prevalent it is, and where it is accepted. Here is what I found:

(1) There are two types of surrogacy: the *traditional*, where a woman gets artificially inseminated with the father's sperm and then gives the baby to the couple after delivery. The surrogate mother is the baby's biological mother because it was her egg that was fertilized by the father's sperm. *Gestational* where the woman of the couple's egg is harvested by IVF, fertilized with a sperm from the father, and placed as subsequent embryo into a gestational surrogate's uterus. The surrogate has no genetic ties to the baby.

(2) Most couples that settle on using surrogacy do so because of problems related to the uterus, such as deformities, hysterectomy, conditions such as heart disease that preclude getting pregnant, attempts at unsuccessful IVFs after miscarriages, and recent social changes in same-sex unions. Seldom does one hear about vanity or preserving physical attributes from edema, stretch marks, and the risks of pregnancy as the reasons for surrogacy.

(3) There are many ways to go about finding an appropriate surrogate mother, whether traditional or gestational. Family and friends or an agency established in making necessary and appropriate arrangements can be avenues for the propositions sought by all parties. How to choose the appropriate surrogate is also very important.

There are some states in the US where surrogacy is codified and allowed. It is illegal in four states—in New York, New Jersey, Washington, and Michigan—and in the District of Columbia. There is no uniform law or restrictions in the other states, and it becomes almost a part of the arrangement process to have the surrogate mother from a state and have the baby delivered in a hospital where surrogacy is not prohibited. The practice is illegal in Canada and some European countries such as Germany, France, Italy, Portugal, and Spain while in the UK, Denmark, Ireland, and Belgium, the surrogate mother is not paid except for reasonable expenses. While there are many complicated questions and the legal ramifications are not addressed (such as how much the surrogate mother is paid if she is, whether she has to pay taxes on the payments made, what tests are required of the surrogate mother as well as the couple seeking surrogacy), Reuters reported in March of 2013 that despite the issues encountered in surrogate pregnancies, the practice is on the rise. Seventy-one percent of people polled support surrogacy, and when it is reduced to gender, 73 percent of women and 69 percent of men approved of the existing tradition.

For Therese, it was her sister Marie who volunteered to be the surrogate mother. She fulfilled all the requirements of being one: not only was it a favor to her younger sister, she had her husband warmed up to the idea, her two children and the family chorusing in unison. Cornell, as the child was called, was a gestational child and became a part of the Custer clan. Marie, by her demeanor, did not think of her uterus as being the incubator of her nephew but rather altruism to a blood relative fettered by inability to get pregnant.

It has been more than four decades since we encountered and interacted with the family. At times, we exchange old and new pleasantries when we get to see each other, which is not very often. And each time we see them, we are always reminded of how fortunate we have been not to face the prospect of surrogacy. But I still relish the idea—which now is impractical—of having enough children to field a basketball team.

> *Being a parent wasn't just about bearing a child. It was about bearing a witness to life.*
>
> *—Jodi Picoult, American writer*

Weight Control

I am always fascinated by the different types of diet hawked every time I turn on my television. It grabs your attention during commercial breaks—the time when stations manage to stay on air and keep their broadcasting alive—by promising that you would lose weight so quickly in a short period of time by subscribing and buying their merchandise. Some even tell those glued to their pitch that it is not necessary to go through measuring the food shipped, counting calories, or weighing yourself in, worries that are necessarily associated if you are about catching the declared end result. I always see Marie Osmond and Nutrisystem, when she extols the virtues of the recent fad. I do not mind seeing her every time she pops up on screen with her sculpted face and svelte figure courtesy of her makeup department and the diet explosion she mentions all the time. But truth be told, I have not seen her in person nor dragged myself to her show with her brother Donny for the seventeen years they have been appearing at the Flamingo, although I heard it was really that good and entertaining. Maybe someday, I will. Neither was Oprah Winfrey when she became a spokesperson for Weight Watchers when she plunked $43.5 million of her hard-earned money in October 2015, now estimated to be $400 million. Her weight has swung like a yoyo, from a size that graced the cover of her magazine to one that showed her upper peninsula. I heard she likes and eats bread like crazy but has mercilessly adhered to the Free Style program though it is, in the words of a disciple, one of the 1.1 million subscribers, "difficult and annoying." She says that Weight Watchers is "less counting and more enjoying," a tag line almost similar to Marie Osmond's exhortation in her commercial. I also see the pitch by weight-loss guru Jenny Craig, who temporarily disappeared from consciousness, staging a virtual and visual comeback with her Rapid Rewards plan that promises a weight loss of twenty pounds after spending anywhere from $1,400 to $2,000 over a ten-week program. It is believed to be "the best way" to shed off those excess pounds anyone carries in his or her midsection. If some skepticism to this claim exists, it is directed at the belt line of the pants previously worn by believers. I think I can go on starvation, spending less on groceries than this monthly average, and still lose the twenty pounds.

You notice though after seeing these commercials over and over again that the second these diets and the delectable foods that accompany them hit the airwaves, *exercise* is always mentioned as part of the equation—that without it, the calories (are they actually reduced per serving?) are unburned and gravitate to areas of the body, notably the midsection, and become not pleasingly undesirable. It leads me to believe that weight loss cannot be attained by diet alone sans the exercise, which occupies a small molecule in many diet pitches. Exercise must share an equal billing to the regimen of staying within the boundaries of weight established by those who measure someone's basal metabolic rate and declare whether one is overweight or not.

In the early seventies when undergoing my surgical training, I was taught that rapid weight loss was not ideal for the human anatomy and its organs that subsequently become pilfered by this change in metabolic alacrity. Through the concept of tinkering with the organ in the gastrointestinal system most involved in weight gain or loss, namely the stomach, many surgical operations over the years have been devised to modify its absorptive and nutritional capacity. I was involved as a junior in a hierarchical pole in a research and operative procedure called 4-14, otherwise named Payne procedure, connecting four inches of small bowel from the ligament of Treitz to fourteen inches of the twenty-one feet of small intestine. The bypassed segment became a "blind loop," and though the patient subsequently lost weight, the metabolic complications that ensued after many years finally became the terminal events that ended the procedure. Many procedures have now been tried: some true and effective, some not, from Mason's vertical banded gastroplasty, to duodenal switch and bilio-pancreatic diversion, sleeve gastrectomy to the more popular and effective Roux-en-Y limb gastroplasty (RYGBP). In several attempts that weight gain and obesity were related to the diet, wiring the jaw shut was temporarily made a focus of this unrestricted behavior. This was eventually thrown into the heap of ineffective approaches to a problem that now has become an epidemic called obesity.

The impetus for the uptick in the weight reduction diets and the not-too-often mentioned *exercise* associated with these diet plans have been the recent surge and increase in the overweight and obesity problems in the country. Among adults, one in three have varying degrees of overweight and obesity. In children and adolescent group ages 2–19, one in six were considered to be obese or overweight. As a consequence, type 2 diabetes related to obesity and being overweight has become a health issue at the forefront today, together with other medical conditions such as high blood pressure, gallstones, and joint problems. These statistics have increased the push for minimally invasive weight-loss surgery to reverse the trend now prevalent among the young, whose weight gain has been attributed to eating habits, physical inactivity, sleep habits, access to active endeavors, computer and smartphone addiction, or genes and medical conditions. To those that have undergone the minimally invasive gastric endoscopic procedure and who have regained their health status, it is hard to argue that undergoing it together with diet and exercise was not worth the expense and the effort. Reducing the size of the stomach and per the National Health Institute statistics, the mortality rate was reduced by 23–40 percent, and remission from type 2 diabetes of 36 percent over a ten-year period, is a health implication that cannot be ignored.

The diet with the glitzy commercials cannot be standalone as a way to reduce the unnecessary weight gain temporarily. Neither is exercise alone. The two must always be mentioned together, as in some of the commercials I have seen. Though it has always driven many to become gym rats in the course of having a lithe and fat-free physique, I am of the impression that many of them engage as well in consuming more salads and diets devoid of carbs and fats. There are also many, young and old alike, who pound the walkway lanes early in the morning or late in the evening in the hope the exercise allows them to reap the benefits of activity without the associated cost of siding with Marie Osmond, tempting as it is. But weight produced by exercise alone is not a predictor of the advantages or disadvantages it brings even in the presence of a trainer. It reminds me of my friend Freddie, a pediatrician who did not have a single ounce of excess fat in his body, played tennis every other day, and hit the gym after office hours every day. He was found dead from heart attack while exercising at the gym. His classmate, also named Fred, went to the golf course daily, had a stroke that eventually resulted in his nurse-wife becoming a widow. Olympians and jogging gurus like Jim Ryun fell and succumbed while engaged in an exercise he espoused, as did the head of cardiology department and husband of a well-known lawyer and weekly TV host for strange inheritance. I heard that he subsequently survived.

The value of both good diet and beneficial exercise is not new. Jack LaLanne, the famed fitness innovator who started with interminable servings of ice cream until he started a fitness craze in 1936, subsequently landing him a TV gig, much like Winfrey or Osmond in their diet commercials, preached the lifestyle before the measured diet and exercise of Richard Simmons or that of Jane Fonda. To prove the value of exercise, he swam handcuffed and shackled at age seventy, towing seventy rowboats from Queens Way Bridge in Long Beach harbor to Queen Mary anchored one mile away, something that I am sure I will never attempt as I know that my drowning will ensue. This is one of his many feats unequaled to this day. Performing his daily workout routine, he died at age ninety-six from respiratory failure.

I haven't tried the many diet fads suddenly raging on TV. It is not because that I do not believe in their purported effect and efficacy as much as I thought of Mac Davis, who once said as I attended his concert many years ago, that all this diet and exercise are not really necessary if we just pay attention to the two most important orifices in our body. One is the inlet that is unrestricted, and the outlet is smaller and autonomically controlled by what we put in. The excess is trapped in the middle. As a surgeon, I found the wisdom of his observation, casual as it might have seemed, believable. By the way, Mr. Davis was a mop-haired singer from West Texas who, at one time, had his own TV show and was known for his jingles on the spot, which I remembered included something about diet.

Enough said.

It matters not what your age is, or your physical condition; if you obey nature laws, you can be born again.

—Paul C. Bragg (who opened the first health food in the nation in 1920)

Professions

Rudyard Kipling was a British writer, an author of short stories, a poet and a novelist noted for his tales of British soldiers in India and his tales for children. His elegant and sweeping words in his novels and poetry, his imaginative storytelling in his celebration of British imperialism as a colonizing power in the Far East, specifically India, where he was born and where he spent most of his adult life, earned him the 1907 Nobel Prize in literature, which he accepted though he turned down many honors offered him like the Poet Laureate and the Order of Merit, even declined a knighthood which would have appended Sir to his name. His poem "If" has always been a source for everyone, me included, of inspiration and motivation of daily living that present-day gurus articulate in different forms of alliterations in their speeches, seminars, and books to stimulate their present audiences.

But it was the opprobrious sense he gave into what is the oldest profession in the world that made me think about the subject in which various professions vied for and claimed the reputation of being the oldest. In his book, *On the City Wall*, he wrote about Lalun, an Indian prostitute, a member of "the most ancient profession in the world." The phrase then acquired its universal meaning after World War I, substituting and dropping the other professions claiming the dubious accolade. The toolmaker that originated 2.6 million years ago in Gona, Ethiopia, the hunter/butcher disputed but estimated to have originated in Tanzania over 1.8 million years ago, the artist whose sketches 67,000 years ago were found in caves in Spain were some of the professions laying claim to being the first and the oldest. There are others—the farmer, musician of ancient era, the storyteller, the builder continue to claim the mantle of legitimacy to clothe themselves in.

Where was my profession then in this pecking order and the attendant genealogy it evolved from? I understand that the present-day surgeons, whose brotherhood I claim to be a member of, originated in the Middle Ages when barbers in small towns who cut hair performed simple operations such as setting fractures or pulling teeth and emerged as a new type of craftsmen. It has been a long way from development as it is today, from the use of wine or honey or willow bark in wounds to prevent infection, to the ancient Egyptians or Greeks who dominated the art of healing nonetheless with ideas that made sense then but are considered aliens today. Herophilus, Galen, da Vinci, Vesalius, Pare, Lister, Hunter, and many more through the centuries to come became pioneers in what is a profession in today's health care industry. As many as there are designations today as *professions*, the "trustworthy" factor trend and survey always come as a measure of what the public thinks. In a British poll survey, family physicians came in at 89 percent followed by schoolteachers, law enforcement, and judges, who scored 70 percent. Here in the United States, in an annual Gallup poll on honesty and ethical standards in 2017, nurses topped again the list of twenty-two professions for the past sixteen years, at 82 percent, while doctors, at 65 percent, polled fourth, next to schoolteachers (third) and military officers (second). I assume that even though my craft may not be the oldest, I prefer to be included in the list called "doctors" or "physicians."

Most parents want their children to be what they are. If they happen to be engineers, or lawyers, doctors or career military, children are guided and directed toward these professions once they think of what to become in the future. Parents that never obtained a higher education other than the lower grades or are fortunate enough to finish high school feel an unabashed pride for any of their children that enter and exit the portals of higher learning with a diploma in hand. I was never encouraged to be what I would become although I was tacitly supported by my parents in any profession I so chose. Growing up, I wanted to be a man of the cloth, reciting Latin as an altar boy though not erudite enough to understand its meaning. I responded to the quiet intonations of the priest at mass when parishioners and the supplicants whispered their own prayers during the service, only to murmur the answer when the celebrant of the mass turned around to face them briefly during the pre-Vatican II ritual. On Sundays, I rode with Father Palma, who at that time was made the parochial vicar of the 300-year-old town church when he visited the sick members of his congregation. Imagine his surprise and despair when I changed my mind after he has enrolled me in a seminary to tell him that seeing Dr. Ben Casey and Dr. Kildare intrigued me to follow a different pathway. I have not seen him since I went to the city to obtain and engage in this profession that I eventually landed in. I think to this day that he failed his bishop and his God delivering me, a prospect to become a disciple of the faith that he was.

There are today many that identify themselves as members of a profession minted by changing times long after the Stone Age of burr holes, cave paintings and sketches, and empires that once dominated the earth. There are now cartoonists, filmmakers, editors, pundits and so-called experts, newsreaders, anchors, reporters, and yes politicians. But it was Rudyard Kipling's direct reference to Lalun's "most ancient profession" that became a euphemism for the morals of today, a phrase whose meaning is easily understood and used to describe those who ply and admit openly their affiliation with the oldest profession.

I consider myself old, but I take pride in saying that my gender was not a subject of a certain author and novelist's idea when he wrote in a biblical reference the book in which Lalun was a famous character.

> *Your profession is not what brings home your weekly paycheck, your profession is what you're put on earth to do, with such passion and such intensity that it becomes spiritual in calling.*
>
> *—Vincent Van Gogh, Post-impressionist painter*

Inheritance

Forbes, that veritable family-controlled magazine published bi-weekly that has a circulation of close to a million readers, came out this year with its annual list of 400 wealthiest Americans. It is a list where every entrepreneur, present, past, and future, aspires to be included as a badge of success in what the market sector brings to someone's business. Seventeen billionaires fell off the list while fifteen made it to the top, pushing the cutoff from being included to a net worth of $ 2.1 billion. Sixty-four inherited their wealth, while the majority, 269 of them, were "self-made." The richest person, Jeff Bezos, is worth $100 billion, surpassing Bill Gates' twenty-four-year run at the top. Most of them have established their own philanthropic foundations, espousing a particular cause now that they can afford to give away much of their riches. It has been said that once you reach this stratospheric atmosphere, you won't bat an eyelash with a million-dollar loss or gain in a day a volatile and capricious market deals with shares or stocks that you own. Although I am not aware of how *Forbes* does its ranking, whether it digs into the entrepreneur's finances that are available in the public domain or scrupulously follows up on how their investments are doing in the stock market or interviews in private the financials of people it has under consideration, I won't dispute their ranking. Next year would be another day.

While sharing their newfound wealth to the underprivileged members of the society by establishing a charitable foundation as a vehicle for giving, the motivation of decreasing or avoiding the tax consequences should not be construed as the only reason for the philanthropy. There is also the process of holding on to and preserving the assets by those who earned them by passing them on to the legal heirs or beneficiaries, through wills or trust or other instruments not in conflict with the law. This is called *inheritance* following the owner's death. In 2018, this means that an individual can leave $5.6 million to heirs, $11.2 million for married couples without paying federal or gift tax. For the richest Americans, it means doling out more, spreading the largesse, which can be a product of birthright, business savvy or acumen and hard work. Some of the wealthiest individuals like Bill and Melinda Gates or Warren Buffett have willed almost half of their assets to philanthropic endeavors than leaving their whole assets to their legal heirs. In *Death of a Salesman*, Arthur Miller's play considered one of the best plays of the twentieth century, Willy Loman, who in the end committed suicide, despaired about leaving nothing of material inheritance to his sons. The ethos of Willy has never been a cause for any rancor in our family. Our parents from the very beginning disclosed to us that there would be no inheritance except for the college education they assiduously provided for the thirteen of us.

The myriad of probative steps required to make the inheritance legal and the complications simple and understandable are the functions of the executor and the estate lawyer. The executor offers the will for probate, distributes the property to the heirs and beneficiaries, protects the assets of the estate, and pays the debts of the estate. The estate lawyer, typically a state-licensed attorney, assists clients in drafting and implementing documents, wills, and trusts of the benefactor.

Inheritance as it is presently understood refers to its legal definition as what a person receives from a decedent provider. But it also means a mechanism whether by laws of descent, other fields or methods, what another (like an offspring) gets from his or her ancestors, somatic or a trait, phenotype, or genotype that makes a person unique. It is acquiring the features and behavior of a class by another class. For instance, I inherited from my father wavy hair, brown skin, and a little bit of being a hoarder of past records, from my mother a penchant for cleanliness and order that almost borders on being an obsessive-compulsive disorder. Unless my blood type changes (which is very rarely caused by suppression or addition caused by factors such as infection or autoimmune diseases) I remain a universal recipient belonging to blood group AB having both A and B antigens on the surface of my red blood cells, but my plasma does not contain the antibodies (IgM) against antigen A or B. While I do not know which one of my parents has the A or B antigen that was passed on to me, I am confident that I inherited the contributions from both of them. An occasion to take advantage of this benefit has never materialized, and I hope that it never will in my lifetime. My brothers and sisters inherited some but not all characteristics and physical attributes that I would imagine passed on to my parents from other family generations. A close observation of every single one of us would probably lead one to know subsequently that we all come from the same family tree.

In modern parlance, inheritance of five or six types (single, multilevel, multiple, hierarchal, and hybrid or multipath) connotes a different application to the computer and Internet world. I am not a computer geek, so don't ask me the definitions of each. All I know is that *Forbes* will come out again next year, in a rite of autumn, with a list of the 400 wealthiest Americans among a population of 340 million. I already know it does not include me, as my name has never been on someone else's list.

> *The best inheritance a parent can give to his children is a few minutes of their time each day.*
>
> —*Unknown*

Smartphones

I have been told and reminded often that the very first rule of being a good conversationalist is knowing how to listen. Or as my friend jokingly says, "Don't talk while I am interrupting." Though it is sometimes hard to rein ourselves in when someone is talking, especially when an idea or comment comes in the middle of someone else's sentence, it is always a sign of politeness that we are made to hold back our interjection. It is an art of conversation that is fundamental as a tool of communication. We disseminate our own ideas or comments and what we know about recent or past events, convey our thoughts (not that they matter), participate in discussions about burning issues of the day, or even gossip why Joe left his children or his family. The subjects of conversation could be held anywhere, any place, be it in a dimly lit corner of a restaurant, a hallway, on a kitchen table, pushing a stroller with an uninterested kid in a park, or in the comfort of an expansive living room. After all, the ability to speak in a language we are accustomed to, verbalize our visions, and communicate with another person is what distinguishes us humans from the other living organisms in the present-day strata.

These days, however, not only social scientists and psychologists but also everyone else including myself, realizes that conversation is beginning to be lost and replaced by zombie-like silence among the denizens of the modern world. People now are preoccupied with the slabs of plastic and metal called smartphones, which are glued to their hands every place they go, oblivious to the neighbors, friends, or strangers who form the cadre of their everyday lives. Not only adults but also the young generation now check their device immediately on waking up or before turning in for the night as if these newfound activities if not performed, adversely affect their daily existence. While the usefulness of the smartphones in today's environment is beyond question, it nevertheless brought, among other things, the obsolescence of conversation as we know it. The spontaneity, the laughter, physicality of the human touch, the jokes interspersed with wide sweeping gestures of the hands, now are seldom seen as expressions of the human mind. Think of a couple who walk into a restaurant, sit down, order from the menu cards, and while waiting, do not engage verbally in what was their day like but talk silently with messages punched from their smartphones forever attached to their upper limbs. And while you are engrossed in some applications downloaded in your smartphones, you continually ignore the stranger sitting beside you who might be willing to engage in some form of banter rather than the attention you struggle to give to your phone. It is a far cry from my late father-in-law, who after a short interaction came back to tell us almost everything he had fished out from someone he did not know but was able to strike up a conversation amiably. He would even know the name of the new acquaintance he just met.

The term *smartphone* was first coined in 1995, a year after IBM's bulky Simon prototype developed by Frank Canova in 1992 made a splash in a computer trade show. The model was then refined into not only receiving cellular calls but also receiving faxes and e-mails. Ericsson R380 touchscreen and released in 2000 was the first device that was marketed as a smartphone. Since then, smartphones underwent several modifications, upgrades, and additions by several computer companies, notably these days Samsung and Apple, which have dominated the market for the past few years. There have been and are still involved, several companies carving a market share of the worldwide and vast demand for the digital device, which has, to date, reached more than a billion users. A smartphone is a mobile phone, a mobile mini-computer supported by wireless communication protocol, Internet capabilities, several software applications that come with video and camera systems, storage, different sensors, and other features not available or known in the past but recently adopted today as part of one's social identity. Whether it thrives on an operating platform like Android or iOS, the fact is that the smartphone has become a necessity in our lives and has spawned many ancillary and support companies and stores today.

With the advent of modern technology comes the price that the society inevitably has to pay. And nowhere is there more than what we normally hold as components of human culture such as communication, conversation, opening the pages of a book, or writing a letter with our own scrawling penmanship to greet or say hello to a friend. These activities have been replaced by the conveniences of modern-day devices, of which a smartphone is one that delivers instant gratification to the many who post online on social media, conversing and sending texts instantaneously or e-mails, shopping without ever stepping in a mall, reading a developing story and a news item at the expense of shuffling to Page Six of print media. And many more, like the risk of being apprehended or worse, losing life or limb texting while driving.

Needing more mobility than was afforded by a call pager, I plunked a considerable sum on the first mobile phone in the market. The price for someone like me was steep, but nevertheless I got my hands on the Motorola DynaTac 8000X in 1984 and became one of the customers who was a proud member of a chorus whose only hymn was the phrase "Look what I got." It was big and heavy and was baptized the Brick, what with its weight of about two pounds and a battery that lasted for a mere thirty minutes every time. Its usefulness lasted me only a year when, tired of lugging it around everywhere I went, I gave it up and reverted to the old reliable pager even though when it beeped I had to search for another phone to return my call. I still have the old albatross. It must be worth its weight in gold by now (although I have not checked it out), considering that at one time, it was a part of technological history. I have always been a geek, keeping my eyes focused on what is new, which leads me to admit that I presently own a recent edition of a smartphone, most of the applications I really do not need.

I do not want to blame the present predicament as the loss of conversational proclivity on smart phones alone. But its ubiquitous availability and presence among us and the continuous improvements and evolution every six or so months, together with other computing devices, have made it irresistible to own or have one. I suppose I will be one forever addicted to it.

> *Your cell phone has already replaced your camera, your calendar, and your alarm clock. Don't let it replace your family.*
>
> —Anonymous

Karaoke

On February 10, 2010, the *New York Times* published a feature article by Norimitsu Onishi about Rodolfo Gregorio, a Filipino barber who, after a day's work at his shop and a glass of beer, belts among the patrons of the local bar "My Prayer" by the Platters, followed by songs by Tom Jones and Engelbert Humperdinck. One song he stayed away from and he had stopped singing was Frank Sinatra's "My Way." The song has become a favorite standard for many years at bars in the country. But sung the way it should be sung, with its melody not out of tune and unadulterated lyrics is what the crowd demands and expects from any attempt to stand up, grasp the microphone, and sing what has become close to an anthem. It is a song sung more often than other songs. Singing off-key or deviations have resulted in fistfights that have become deadly; deaths have ensued from disputes that erupted from habitués that have low tolerance for bad singing, dubbing the incidents "My Way" killings. As infamous as the Philippines has become for karaoke bar killings, incidents of similar nature have happened in China, South Korea, Japan and have spread to the West, including such cities as Seattle and San Diego and other countries that have embraced this cultural phenomenon.

Karaoke is a form of interactive entertainment with lyrics of a popular song that change color as an amateur singer using a microphone attached to a screen sings along. The prototype machine was invented in 1971 by a Japanese drummer, Daisuke Inoue, who developed the idea when his guests asked him to provide recordings of his performances so they could sing along, a feature of Mitch Miller's sing-along on his NBC TV show *Sing Along with Mitch* (sans a vocalist), which ran from 1961 to 1966. In Asia with countries like China, Cambodia, and the Philippines, the machine was known as KTV (karaoke television) and because initially the invention was not patented, many companies that subsequently followed made revolutionary and technical changes dictated by the music industry, portability of the equipment, the ease of use by entertainers, musicians and amateur singers being one of the requirements. It was a Filipino, Roberto del Rosario who filed a patent in 1975 for a karaoke machine the Sing Along Machine that he developed. Early on, the technological modification and incorporation of newer additions to the karaoke machine did not result in increased sales and success in the Western markets until lately, the "bizarre" social phenomenon caught on; with the popularity it now has worldwide, the global market is estimated in the billions of dollars. Almost four decades after its first introduction as a simple box, technology has enhanced this onetime "sinister" contraption with enhancements that give it a stereo system and a home theater quality. It is and can be a permanent fixture now in bars, lounges, in impromptu rooms and conference halls, cruise lines, and in homes, where privacy trumps an unwanted audience and publicity. International competitions in Europe, Finland and in US places like Las Vegas and Times Square in New York City have been hosted by various producers.

While social life has since included people who are persuaded to sing and those willing to perform, the widespread popularity of karaoke has sometimes created problems in some venues aside from the well-known rage engendered by the song "My Way." The feeling evoked by some of the lyrics of a song, the restrictions of licensing agreements from record producers and music houses and the perception that some songs offend other ethnic or religious groups, have led to some karaoke songs banned or prohibited in some places. Songs like Katy Perry's "Roar," Justin Timberlake's "Can't Stop the Feeling," Lady Gaga's "Edge of Glory" (considered "too vulgar" in China), and of course, "Holiday" by Madonna, whose appearance has been banned for various reasons around the world, were some of the ditties purged from the karaoke list. This has not prevented, however, Philippine president Rodrigo Duterte, who on November 11, 2016, sang a duet on a karaoke with Malaysia's prime minister Najib Razak before sitting down to tackle diplomatic issues between the two countries. Anything to influence a diplomatic initiative. By the way, Mr. Daisuke Inoue from Hyogo, Japan, whom I presume is in his late seventies, received in 2014 the Ig Nobel Prize, for his karaoke invention. The award during the fourteenth annual ceremony was given to ten individuals for their unusual or trivial achievements each autumn at the Sanders Theatre in Harvard. It is given by Nobel laureates, although the prize is a parody of the Swedish Nobel awards, the *Ig* a pun on the word *ignoble*. He was cited for his invention, "an entirely new way for people to tolerate each other." Reportedly, being a musician, his rendition of "I'd Like to Teach the World to Sing" received such a long standing ovation that even the Nobel Prize laureates responded with a chorus of "Can't Take My Eyes off You."

I was once a president of a glee club that competed intramurally with different groups in the university. My pipes were in the tenor range, of which there were a few in my section. We won a few medals during my term, when karaoke was not a local or a global entity. Nowadays though, with the advent of modern technology, I bought a karaoke machine and, with it, many song selections, a number of which rate my performance in the high eighties but never in the realm of perfection. My voice is an octave lower these days, the effect of vocal cords that have become gradually stiffer. So even if I relish the hope of making it to the audition of *The Voice*, I would rather watch the show than face the music with karaoke or a live backup band. You would not find me either entering a karaoke bar belting Bette Midler's "Wind Beneath My Wings," which I heard was banned. And I would not attempt to hum a chord of Frank Sinatra's "My Way."

I still want to live and look forward to a longer life.

Karaoke bars combine two of the nation's greatest evils: people who shouldn't drink with people who shouldn't sing.

Tom Dreesen, American stand-up comedian and actor

Everyone hates being humiliated. Yet karaoke still exists.

Lotto

Primm is a small town along Interstate 15 between Southern Nevada and California. It is a border town 42 miles from Las Vegas or 263 miles from the city hall in downtown Los Angeles. On most Friday nights and holidays, cars with California license plates clog the interstate highway toward Las Vegas, populating the hotels and casinos that line the 4-mile Strip, crowding the local citizens of the surrounding communities, who would rather retreat to the peripheral station casinos and restaurants. The town is actually part of Nevada's Clark County, although the small side of it straddles California, the border state. For those residents of California who find it worthwhile the travel to avail themselves of the inexpensive amenities that Primm's budget-friendly attractions provide, the weekend or the short holiday trip ends there. But for the residents of Nevada, where any form of lottery, whether local, statewide, or national, is nonexistent or not allowed, Primm and its local convenience store on the California side becomes a pilgrimage city, especially when Mega Million and the Powerball lotto reach stratospheric heights of riches available to a ticket holder who has a molecular chance of winning.

The lottery has become a national consortium of forty-four states across the country that participate in a multistate operation. Puerto Rico, a commonwealth of the US, actually started lottery mania in 1934 which was then followed by subsequent states of the union. The introduction of scratch cards in 1970 in individual lotteries became another source of state revenue. It is akin to a numbers game where three to six numbers result in a jackpot dictated by the numbers of the game. Mississippi recently legalized US lottery this year with ticket sales to start in early 2019. In 2018 before the year ends, Americans spent $77.7 on various lotteries, an increase of $5 billion in 2017 with the recent Powerball jackpot winning over a billion dollars. The acceptance of what was initially a form of entertainment in the earlier colonial days to today's state source of revenue to fund individual states' programs and initiatives has been the reason for those legislatures to pass the creation of these lotteries. Maine, New Hampshire, and Vermont started it all in 1986, and in 1988, six states and the jurisdiction of the District of Columbia formed what is known today as Powerball. In 1996, six other states created the Big Game, now known as Mega Millions. Although Powerball and Mega Millions in 2009 had an agreement to cross-license the two games jointly in forty-four states, both have different administrative bodies. Puerto Rico offers Powerball but not Mega Millions.

The unholy alliance that grew between the gaming industry and the anti-gaming people who still consider lotteries a form of gambling, and the corruption that followed the creation of lotteries, have six other states decline Powerball or Mega Millions within their borders. They don't even have state lotteries in their system. Alabama, Alaska, Hawaii, Mississippi, though, recently relented and abolished the prohibition—Nevada and Utah have their state constitutions, religious denominations, and/or political reasons for having the state legislatures not signing on the expansion of this option. In Nevada, the decision by the state legislature fifty years ago to ban lotteries was reinforced by the Nevada Gaming Control Board and the gaming industry to just make Nevada a casino state to this day. It allows charitable drawings however by local clubs like those held by Boy Scouts, schools, and Elks' Clubs although it still needs approval of the events by the gaming board.

For those who believe that the chance of a lifetime involves having the millions and the billions of a single lottery ticket, heading out of a state where the lotto is banned and going to another where it is sold is just a temporary inconvenience in exchange for the comforts the jackpot brings. While to many, participation in a lottery is a regressive activity, as it involves mostly people who consider themselves average to poor in the wealth category, the lure of going up the scale is too much to ignore. So people in Nevada close to the California border drive to Primm Valley Lotto Store on the other side of town and stand up in long lines for hours on end just for a Quick Pick or a ticket where the significance of the chosen numbers is known only to the buyer. Otherwise, one can drive to a ninety-mile stretch to Arizona for the privilege of having that closely held ticket. Forgotten during the rush to the convenience store are the recommended other attractions. Primm is known mostly for the fashion outlets, the small casinos and hotels, and the golf courses, where a friend of mine one time had a rattlesnake guarding his errant ball.

Living in Texas for almost four decades before I migrated to the Silver State, I easily procured a Powerball or Mega Millions ticket from small convenience stores scattered along the many intersections I negotiate going to work. I seldom engaged in getting out of my car for a minute or two to buy my way to unimaginable riches, the odds of winning being projected to be somewhere between one in eight to nine hundred million. I always remind my friends, my wife included, about the odds and that spending a buck or two is like throwing away your remaining resource into the wind. I always get a retort of "Tell that to the person who won," which immediately makes me screech to stop my plausible comment.

There have been many stories written and features shown about the lives of people who one day found themselves lucky among the many whose dreams did not transform into reality. Mostly the winners are ordinary working people, those we always say that the jackpot could not have been won by a more deserving person. (Who has seen the rich like Bill Gates or Warren Buffett fall in line to add to the billions they already have?) In the long run, however, the newfound fortune wrought havoc and misery in the lives of the lotto winners. The millions in cash that suddenly overwhelmed them and spending it like there was no end to it, friends coming out of the woodwork, claiming to be forgotten relatives, or plain stupidity of someone with sudden wealth are some of the reasons by the winners that winning is, after all, not everything or the only thing.

I already have a plan that is devoid of all the mistakes and misfortunes of those fortunate enough to be the recipient of the lotto largesse. It is in place. That is, if I buy a ticket in Primm and am lucky enough among the millions nationwide that trek to stores every time that the jackpot becomes stratospheric. The only problem is that I have not gone to Primm and I have not accepted the odds of winning.

I have done the calculation and your chances of winning the lottery are identical whether you play or not.

—Fran Lebowitz, public speaker

I despise the lottery. There is less chance of you becoming a millionaire than there is of getting hit on the head by a passing asteroid.

—Brian May, CBE, British guitarist, musician, and cofounder of the band Queen

Sleep

As much as it has been suggested that to maintain a good mental and physical health, positive well-being, regeneration of the brain, and recovery after hectic waking hours of activities, I need and have to consistently engage my body in a complex process of suspended state of consciousness and outside awareness for at least eight to nine hours every day. It is called sleep. Like 98 percent of the population, a person needs at least this many hours every night. But I have been, like most people over the years, sleep deprived, incurring what is known today as sleep debt. It all started at the time I was in school burning the midnight oil to commit to memory the many essential points of Christopher's *Textbook of Surgery* as a student and recalling the lessons learned from the mistakes I might have overlooked later in the practice of my craft. The changes in my biological rhythm, I am afraid, have become permanent despite the recommendations of leading sleep researchers of the many techniques to combat the sleep debt, which occasionally results in my dozing off in some seminars or conferences I attend, especially when the subject matter or speaker becomes boring. I am still able to function nevertheless whether or not I am able to cobble up four to six hours of sleep. I do, however, attribute not receiving enough sleep, shorter than I normally have, to environmental influences, such a room that is too hot or cold or bright, interruptions like family members' snores, sleep preferences, or difficulties. Traveling and changes in time zones sometimes upset my circadian rhythm, but the use of modern tools of technology such as headsets and smartphone screens has partially made plane rides across the oceans tolerable.

Though there are multiple factors that affect getting a good sleep like the increased stress in people's lives, the numerous problems encountered daily, fragmented components of work (such as shift work) or leisure, or some medical conditions that cannot be prevented or avoided, the decline from nine to seven hours of sleep, sometimes shorter, has been evident and palpable. More than 75 percent of adult Americans and 25–30 percent of infants and children are thought to suffer from sleep disorder, with inability to either sleep or sleep soundly. This has added, by some estimates, sixteen to seventeen billion dollars in health costs to the government annually. Included in this increasing sleep deprivation are the number of researchers who have continually studied the effects it has on sleep cycle, academic achievement, its variability and the risks it brings, and its impact on various treatments. They have recommended cognitive and behavioral treatments as well as the use of pharmacologic approaches to the disorder often called insomnia. Cognitive behavioral therapy at times has been shown to be very effective, better than a pill such as Ambien in people who change their thought process and behavior to solve their sleeping problems. Although it has been shown that the brain remains active during sleep, most bodily functions, such as blood pressure, body temperature, and breathing rate, are decreased.

There is a group of people who call sleep a waste of time. They constitute about 1–3 percent of the population, have a few hours of sleep (typically four hours or less), and tackle the days without caffeine or taking naps. They are called natural sleepers or early birds because they get up shortly after midnight, are high achievers, generally energetic and outgoing, seldom tired, and find more important and interesting things during day than nighttime. This group is hard to find and therefore small studies have so far been done to study them. Besides, they do not consider themselves having a disorder and thus they seldom go to sleep clinics or centers. Call them an aberration, but they do exist. In 2009, Dr. Ying-Hui Fu from the University of California–San Francisco was part of a research team that discovered hDEC2, a genetic variation in two subjects of their study. This resulted in some potential candidates to be included in a study by neurologists and sleep scientists about the true nature of short sleepers, most of whom so far were found to have different circadian rhythms, have upbeat moods, be thinner than the average person, and have a high tolerance to physical pain. This scarce group's subset of sleep disorder does not appeal to me even with the positive attributes they are found to possess.

Knowing that not getting the right amount of sleep results in the prevailing concept of serious physical, emotional, and mental well-being of others; a family member has slowly but progressively developed what I thought was a sleep disorder that selfishly I had to deal with day in and day out, leading me to bring her for two consecutive nights to a sleep disorder center to diagnose the problem. Having identified what the reason was that prevented me from getting some shuteye during the night with the quarters I shared with her, the treatment prescribed was so effective that I had to pause sometimes to check the subsequent quiet relaxation she nocturnally had, to make sure she was still breathing and alive. Better still, the contraption prescribed by the cardiologist was so small and portable that putting it in a small bag and bringing it wherever we go has been very practical. Even her nightmares that occasionally woke me up eventually disappeared.

The longest time that someone did not have any sleep was in 1964, when for eleven days, Randy Gardner set this record. Although this may sound surprising, it was reported on a different occasion that the longest noted sleep deprivation was when a contestant pulled in 18 days, 21 hours, and 40 minutes without a wink on a rocking chair marathon. While the need for a sleep does not decline as I grow older and my ability to pull in 4–5 hours of sleep may be reduced, I do not intend to submit to some contemplated test of whether I can top the records of the individuals who stayed awake. I would rather be fatigued and irritable not having my nightly allotment of 4–5 hours than be upbeat and stimulated by dopamine of an oversleeping mesolimbic pathway.

Do I think of myself as elite, considering that I almost make the hours needed to be a natural sleeper? I am not thin; neither am I devoid of some of the medical conditions inherent supposedly with people who develop and have sleep disorders. For those interested, just wait for the answer after I wake up from my nap.

I love to sleep. Do you? Isn't it great? It is really the best of both worlds. You get to be alive and unconscious.

—Rita Rudner, American comedienne

The worst thing in the world is to try to sleep and not to.

—F. Scott Fitzgerald, American author

Genealogy

Time magazine a few years ago had a picture of an American woman on its cover. It was an amalgamation of phenotype diversity the country was experiencing at that time where the analysis of the population and the composition of the country's future appears to be influenced by immigration and interracial marriages resulting in a mixed ancestry. The underlying projections was that the percentage of white immigrants- those that came from Southern and Eastern Europe which comprised the majority of the present American population will decline in the year 2050 and that the immigrants from Asia and Latin America, especially those from the latter will change the racial and ethnic composition of the US population. This change will have societal and political implications, the thesis continues, with these groups trying to integrate in the prevailing American society while maintaining the cultures and identity of where they came from and the heritage that comes with it. We see it in the past and more so now as the political structure of government is a mixture of racial and mixed-ethnic representation. Thus we now see that the levers of government diverse as the attitudes and the assumptions of the current population which is increasingly multicultural and complex especially for the recent settlers in the United States. The Hispanic and Latino people now comprise 18% of the 327 million total US population according to the recent US Census, African-Americans amounting to 12.7%, while the others, 5.6% from the other geographical areas of the world constitute the remainder of the non-Hispanic whites as Asian- Americans such as Chinese, Filipinos, or Indians. Sixty-four percent of the Caucasians and their descendants still constitute the present majority of the population which as conflicting projections predict will eventually be superseded by a mixed breed of Americans in the years to come. It has always been a closely held truism that a country is enriched by immigrants that eventually settled and formed a nation. America was from the outset a multiethnic and multicultural society, from the early settlers in the seventeenth and eighteenth centuries from Europe, and the indentured peoples from Africa and the Caribbean, and the subsequent displacement and absorption of the indigenous peoples of the discovered continent of North America. But things have moved to the present and while the differing ideology and identities exist in a fluid society such as the United States, changes in a society which is in constant flux are never fixed nor immutable.

I was reminded a few weeks ago about this aspect of racial difference and diversity we are born with, while surfing and finally settling on watching one of the beauty pageants on television. Of the more than a dozen beauty contests held every year, the Miss Universe Beauty Pageant was holding its 67th competition at the Impact Arena in Bangkok, Thailand. Of the 94 contestants, all in their twenties, except for a few who were ethnically noticeable as representatives of their country, the rest all looked phenotypically similar, their demographic origins and where they live indicative of the blur immigration, interracial marriage and ancestry brings. Consider the subsequent winner of the pageant, Catriona Gray who is an Australian citizen born in Cairn, Australia to a Scottish father and a Filipina mother, graduated from a Boston college, representing the Philippines and does not look like a typical Filipina. Or Miss Nepal, Manita Devkota who does not look Nepalese, graduated from a North Carolina university and presently established her domicile in North Carolina. Despite the supercontinent that existed during the Pangaeac age and the expectation that population would all look alike therefore, the shift of land mass occurring in stages 350 million years ago resulting in the formation of present-day oceans and continents and countries with different climates, environments structure, and habitats. More importantly is the typical appearance of the inhabitants of the countries created by these tectonic shifts. Thus, Africans, Chinese, Arabs, Europeans, Asians, etc look differently. While it seems that every one of the contestants tries to be monolithic in appearance and not of the country they represent except for the traditional costume they wear and parade in one segment of the competition, it only is made up of the female gender and a small pie of a society and does not identify with the many that may alter the makeup of a population of a country they want to immigrate, be assimilated and be a part of. I predict that this contest of how we value the pulchritude of women will invariably be altered from now on by the first transgender contestant Angela Ponce promulgated by the country of Spain where she (he) comes from.

Two years ago while attending a wedding in Tennessee to my sister's daughter (my sister is married to an Irish-American), my son who is himself married to a blonde, blue-eyed daughter-in-law, brought in for me and my wife test tubes for us to individually fill up to determine our ancestry composition, maternal and paternal haplogroups, health risks and traits, our ethnic origin from a genetic testing company recently formed, a beneficiary of Watson-Crick DNA discovery. It was no surprise that the results came back and one of them showed that I was almost one hundred percent of Asian/Malayan descent and a smattering of few racial genes which judging from my looks and the color of my skin grossly tell me and anyone else about where my heritage and where I originally came from. In fact, people will recognize me as coming from different race in a country I now call myself a citizen of for half a century. I can not argue with what the molecule shaped like a twisted ladder that James Watson and Francis Crick discovered in 1953 for which they, together with Rosalind Franklin and Maurice Wilkins received the Nobel Price in Physiology in 1962 tell me how my genes came about and how it plays a role in the processes that brought me my son and my daughter. The double helix of nucleotides and the subsequent discoveries of its extensions have contributed to forensic science and the appearance of the future American on the cover of *Time* magazine. Surprisingly, my wife has more ancestry origins in her blood than she could imagine. Where she had progenitors that were Jewish or Chinese was a shock to us all but looking back, there were many of these racial and ethnic groups that in the past and presently were integrated in the society and country where we all came from.

Every time I power the television on, an item detailing the continued saga of people wanting to move to a different landscape for better opportunities that exist somewhere else than where they originally are from or to escape the prevailing and precarious conditions they find themselves in. In effect, if they are successful, they would alter and ultimately change the face of the country they move to. The composition of the population would change.

Having lived here for most of my adult life has contributed to this change in the demographics of the country. My children, grandchildren, nephews and nieces and my relatives have become nondescript faces of the future generations of Americans that eventually make up hopefully the cover of a magazine . Meanwhile I will not wait to change the way I look even though I have been assimilated in a society of Asian –Americans that constitute a small percentage of the US population and which I presently belong.

Even if I wait, it won't happen because I won't be around for a million years.

> *"Genealogy itself is something of a privilege, coming far more easily to those of us for whom enslavement, conquest, and dispossession of our land has not been our lot"*
>
> *- Tom Wise, American Anti-racial activist and writer*

Medical and Surgical Missions

In 1999, the Nobel Peace Prize was awarded to an international medical humanitarian organization. Founded on December 22, 1971, in Paris, France by Bernard Kouchner and Jacques Beres, Medicins Sans Frontieres (Doctors Without Borders) continues to work all over the world, extending volunteer humanitarian medical access to healthcare in more than seventy countries. While the small outfit I have been a part of since 1985, delivering annual and sometimes twice-a-year surgical care to an indigent population limited to a specific part of the world, I felt a sense of unadulterated pride that a fraternity of similar mien and kinship was recognized for a helping hand it extends to the underprivileged deserving of help. I cannot claim the scope of their outreach in conflict zones, in areas where epidemics and natural disasters occur, requiring emergency response, but I have been privy to volunteer work that sometimes requires physical and emotional sacrifice that almost all volunteers of different stripes experience when they undertake voluntary separation from the confines of their comfort zones even temporarily.

There are hundreds of organizations who do mission work, who conduct humanitarian endeavor at no cost to the beneficiaries and are generally devoid of political patronage or color. Some are permanent and continuously, on a regular basis, field teams of volunteers to areas locally and internationally where the need for help arises. Others are spurred by recent disasters such as earthquakes, floods, and tsunamis, and as soon as the situation is controlled and stabilized, recede or become dormant to restructure again for future responses to natural calamities or health crises in some countries. Most of the missionary organizations deploy their activities and resources in the impoverished citizens of Africa, although there are ethnic groups' and church-sponsored medical missions in South America and Asia. Albert Schweitzer, a German that eventually became a French citizen on account of his wife Helene, who was his anesthesiologist in their mission to Gabon, Africa, has become an international symbol, as a missionary who gave up a lucrative doctrinal post in a German evangelical mission espousing St. Paul's eschatology but opted to spread his theology at his own expense in the remote and impoverished area and the underprivileged population of a French colony in Africa. His opinions and concepts over two decades of his life and work in Africa are acknowledged to this day and have become a template for some mission organizations around the globe.

In 1972, a year after the founding of Doctors Without Borders in Paris, the Society of Philippine Surgeons in America was founded and established in the United States under the prevailing set of circumstances then. Though the conditions and situations under which it was founded have changed and are no longer present nowadays, it has continued to exist up to now based on the three legs it stands on, among which are the surgical missions it annually conducts to Third World countries, especially the Philippines. While ethnic in its original composition, it has now become international, with participants coming from the United States, its territories, Canada, and Europe. Its past and present leaders have been recognized with many awards nationally and internationally for the missions it has undertaken. I joined the society in the mid-eighties and have been part of the surgical missions since then. Surgical or medical teams, regardless of whether the member is a physician, nurse, or auxiliary personnel, require a zeal and humanitarian spirit to extend a helping hand to an indigent and deserving population in any country. Pecuniary remuneration for those that signed up generally is not a consideration, for the salaries or reimbursements as far as I am aware of are so miniscule. Most of these missions are funded by wealthy philanthropists, by donations from charitable groups or individuals, by different ethnic or church-based organizations. For those that do it at the expense of their time, talent, and treasure, the desire for the outreach is encompassing. It is a reality to many organizations involved in foreign medical and surgical missions that sometimes these "intrusions" are subtly opposed by the local medical community as well as the government through the ponderous and, most of the time, onerous requirements they impose in conducting these missions. Although there are legitimate reasons for these restrictions, it is really a tacit acceptance of a shortcoming not adequately and timely addressed by a government and the medical community of that given country.

While it is always a necessity to adhere to the requirements of the local government units (LGU) and follow the dictates of the nongovernmental organizations (NGO) and the national government itself to conduct these missions, I was immune and not concerned with the vicissitudes of keeping up to them early on, when all I had to do was signify my intentions of joining the outreach as a fellow of the society. This went on until five years ago, when the untimely demise of the co-chair of the committee and the subsequent resignation of the other after many years of heading the group thrust me and another surgeon from California to head the surgical mission committee. The responsibility of assembling the team, the number of missionaries and the specialties involved, the support group and the auxiliary, the supplies of the mission and where it was going to be delivered, and the logistical arrangements of the local host were things that needed to be attended to for almost a year prior to the event.

But it was all worth it. One can never materially quantify the impact created by these humanitarian sojourns in underdeveloped countries. After all, it is mostly from the highly industrialized and advanced countries that the missionary organizations originate. To see thousands of people ensconced in a gymnasium after a long trip from home, at times sleeping under the mercy of the elements waiting to be seen, processed, and scheduled for surgery for the next few days, gives one pause about why charity halfway around the globe is still a virtuous act of intended consequences. To see someone with a far-advanced tumor, five- or ten-year history of a neglected sore, or a condition that could have been prevented if nipped early in the bud raises more questions for anybody coming in from a place where health care is almost a right rather than a privilege. Of course, the answer could be discerned by the financial depravity that many of these indigent people experience in their daily lives and the inability to seek early medical or surgical attention from health care providers who have a tiered approach to these problems. The medical missionaries, whether in for a long haul or for a short time like the Society of Philippine Surgeons in America, can only perform within the confines and limitations imposed by their host and the venues where they are allowed to operate. The stay becomes a two-way street, the missioners with their expertise and the lectures they give but at the same time absorbing and learning how it is that the local community deals with the problems at hand. Of the cases that no one sees or experiences but common in Third World countries, premier surgical organizations such as the American College of Surgeons have looked into the possibility of having those undergoing surgical training to rotate abroad to broaden their acumen on a global nature. Some medical schools even have far-flung outposts in Africa where some of their medical students and residents go to and spend some time to deliver and at the same time learn the prevalent conditions that the country suffers from. My secondhand knowledge comes from my nephew who, while in residency training, had to spend a few months in Madagascar in Africa, where the GDP per capita is only $934 a year, the ninth poorest country in the Third World.

It is not hard to pull yourself up by your bootstraps for humanitarian endeavor. Going to these missions proves to be a respite from the complexities of dealing with the maze of health care back home. The eleven-year-old child whose left fingers were fused by scars from a burn she suffered and, six years later, were released had a hug that melted my heart as she embraced me, with a rice cake in her hand, cooked by her mother the day we were supposed to leave. But an old man who had to walk seventy kilometers, hoping that his hernia down to his knees could be fixed but could not on the day we were leaving, left ennui among the members of the team. Maybe the next wave of missionaries could attend to him if he showed up on time.

For as long as 795 million in the world don't have enough resources (and 40 percent of the world's population of 8 billion in 2024, as projected by the United Nations Population Reference Bureau), missions to alleviate those unfortunate enough on the other side of the spectrum will continue.

After all, it will never be a perfect world.

> *There is no painkiller as effective as love, no antidepressant as soothing as cheer, no defibrillator as powerful as wisdom.*
>
> *Abhijit Naskar, Time to Save Medicine*
>
> *Life begins at the end of your comfort zone.*
>
> *Mission Trip Quotes*

Television

A few years back, I got a solicitation note from Nielsen wanting to know if I would join their sample of representative households who divulge through their metrics what television programs they were watching whenever they turn their television on. This was followed again by the same note subsequently for the following years. I did not answer any of their requests for audience measurements and their claim of proven methodology, although it might have been an uncivilized way of saying no. But I was zealously into protecting the privacy endangered by letting someone know what programs I was watching at a particular time and then lumping me into a statistic that television networks subscribe to and buy to determine what TV programs they would develop, continue, or stop in specific markets across the country, based on the viewership it captures. Not that I do not care for anyone to know what I generally have my eyes on the telly, because I really do. I might even influence some other viewers about the programs I watch to enhance how smart they can be. But the behemoths of social media such as Facebook, YouTube, and Google are now facing privacy problems here and abroad. And it is not over yet. I suspect that it will go on for some time.

While Nielsen Media Research, which operates the Nielsen ratings, morphed from the time it was founded in the '20s by Arthur Nielsen as a radio programming analysis to what it is now, knowing the viewing habits of 5,000 households across the country and then developing a technologically sophisticated statistical system that TV networks use in determining the advertising rates and programs they would field, some already voiced criticisms about its ratings systems. The rapidly advancing technology such as smartphones, tablets, computers, or other mobile devices where audiences view other video programs that are not tracked by the metrics presently employed by Nielsen and others are being addressed in a comprehensive and alternative metering and electronic methodology. Since 1950, when Nielsen started its network ratings and CBS occupied the number one slot in the last forty-four out of the sixty-five years it has done so, there have been reports that the mainstream media is considering dropping its contract with Nielsen, as the ratings are no longer the reliable measure of viewership they once were. It is a sad commentary that people nowadays seem to be ambivalent and have low regard for the ratings although statistical measurements are used still by the media companies, especially by television, in determining the programs they are going to air and the advertising rates they are going to charge.

Television sets came out in 1927. Two years after that came the Great Depression in the United States, when people were forced to scratch and eke out a living. I was not born until almost two decades later, but my family never owned a set until the late '60s. I always associate one Tuesday my father walked into our house with a seventeen-inch Hitachi television set, carrying it under his armpit as the day that finally ended my mom's odyssey of having thirteen pregnancies in sixteen years, when all the family members, including my prolific father, gathered at night to watch Leonard Bernstein conduct the New York Philharmonic Orchestra and the musical lessons he imparted during his moments at the podium. Vic Morrow was the quintessential combat hero that my father always admired because at one time, he was in the service and World War II. Occasionally, we gave in to my mother's whim of having a wrestling match show, especially if involved women wrestlers. She would get animated by every move by the wrestlers made in the ring. Little did we know that it was all choreographed, until later. And of course, we watched Eric Sevaried, Harry Reasoner, or Walter Cronkite deliver the events of the day in a half-hour newscast. The broadcasts were where we learned about the history of the Third Reich, the Korean War, and the aftermath of the Second World War, and of course, the first man on the moon. Although black-and-white broadcasting ended many years after it first came out and color broadcast began in the mid-1960s, we still held on to the only TV set we had. The television set, which occupied a prominent shelf space in the family living room, was then a black-and-white apparatus with a concave screen and a dial that required you to get off your chair to change to a channel, the numbers of which were limited to what is now labeled as the mainstream media. The largest screen I could remember was twenty-one-inch set, and the television set was as heavy as it was bulky.

It is extremely different today. Technology and the rapid pace of its development gradually changed the set from its original configuration to ones that are designed to be thinner, bigger and have less glare, have high dynamic range, and have 100 percent color volume. There are many models to choose from, with acronyms appended to the models, like OLED (organic light-emitting diode), QLED (quantum light-emitting diode), smart TV, LED, and the older HD1080. And with the increase in TV commercial stations to 1,761 to the proliferation of cable networks and the concomitant number of programs available to choose from, the average consumer like myself is confused whenever I enter an appliance center or turn the TV on nowadays. The screens now are much larger, up to sixty-five inches the last time I wandered around in an appliance center. No longer are the bulky sets that I still have from previous years still with excellent and picture- perfect color accepted as charitable donations for which you can receive an acknowledgment receipt at Salvation Army or Goodwill. I have to make a confession though—I have more of the new TV sets in my house than I really need.

Turning the TV on for an average show of an hour brings in sixteen minutes of commercial advertising and an average of thirty-eight commercials every minute on national television—slightly less from cable networks, of course. Some have avoided what is considered an annoying item from watching a favorite program by subscribing to commercial-free networks like Netflix or going back to the old movie reruns shown on Turner Broadcasting Network. With the increase in networks and hiring pool of newscasters, it is inevitable that biases and the polarity of these anchors and talk show hosts of the so-called mainstream media, both the national and cable networks, have become palpable and brought upfront, and every invited guest on the show is automatically labeled an expert.

It has been said that in an average lifetime, a person spends fifteen years of his/her life watching television. That amounts to more than 140 hours per month and 1,700 hours almost for a year in somebody who lives to about seventy-eight years. I am not that old as yet, but I would not let anyone know what TV programs I watch occasionally, as Nielsen asked me one day. What anyone can tell about me by the sports, newscasts, politics, and history that turn me on, I better leave it as is. It is better that way.

Movie Houses

Albemarle Theatre sits among the line of business establishments on Flatbush Avenue, at the junction of Cortelyou Road. Built in 1921, it was a grand movie house with its wide and ornate stage with its single screen and a grand banquet hall above the auditorium, which was accessed through a side door. In the early '70s, and less than a half-mile from an apartment where I lived, I walked to watch Robert Redford's film *The Sting* and Gene Hackman's *French Connection*. These might not have been the only movies I and my wife and friends watched at the nearby theater. But I have since moved in the late '70s to start a new practice of my craft in the Southwest. I understand it now houses the Kingdom Hall of the Jehovah's Witnesses after a fire in 1984 that closed its door despite the remodeling and renovations of a marquee movie palace. Nostalgic as I am about where I resided and spent part of my formative years in surgery, I have not driven through Flatbush, seen Albemarle and Erasmus High and all the changes I heard about that have come in the decades that followed after I left. I visit Greenwood Cemetery at least once a year in Brooklyn, where my parents and Jim and his wife Zeny are buried, but I skirt passing through downtown and instead get through BQE then to the 24th entrance. I understand that the borough has even built a new basketball arena where the NBA team from New Jersey have become the Brooklyn Nets, that Junior's cheesecake having achieved a well-deserved reputation has expanded to nationwide reach, and Brooklyn Bridge still straddles the East River and has a commanding view of Lower Manhattan.

Progress is a derivative of change. As infrequently as my wife and I have gone to the movies in the many decades that followed after we moved from the city that never sleeps, movie houses have changed from the palatial single-screen performance venues that were used for multipurpose events such as feature films and vaudeville. Many have closed or shuttered, like the grand Casino theater on DeKalb Avenue, which was turned into a high school at the turn of the century. Others no longer occupy a place on main streets or prominent boulevards. Of the remaining performance venues, the Kings theater in Flatbush was renovated and restored to its glory days and made modern by the New York City Economic Development and the Loews Cineplex Entertainment remains a historic relic of a past continuing to survive, with its calendar of shows. Most movie houses are now located inside shopping malls with utilitarian halls, the size of which depends on how many screens are feasibly chopped for the moviegoers. While these modern venues have better sound and projection systems, they haven't catered to what the late Andy Rooney complained about, the length of the commercials and the trailers that precede the featured presentation. People that go to movie houses, he said, want to escape the unnecessary distractions of a person or an outfit selling a product or some service and just want to see the film they went to see and dig into the bag of popcorn or slurp their soda pop.

There are approximately five thousand and seventy cinema sites in the country. Each year, the different studios churn out more movies than can be shown at multiplexes. There are approximately five thousand seven hundred fifty cinema sites in the United States, and with so many movies made, it is always a competition to be a big hit to score the most return on the movie production costs. Last year, there were 563 movies released, 871 in North America and over 2,000 worldwide. The Chinese, while producing more flicks than the United States, can't match box office revenues in the country. And so does India. One of the more recent developments in the movie industry is the advent of subscription services that allow you to watch any genre of film on tiny screens in the comfort and privacy of your home at a time of your own choosing. Whether it is the amount of pyrotechnics that certainly abound in today's movies at the expense of dialogue that tells the story, or the animations of Pixar or Walt Disney that blow up gross box office receipts, or even the documentaries that tell the historical perspective of an event, many companies have latched on to the changing market. Netflix, Hulu, the peripatetic Shoebox, Amazon, and many more are here on the heels of the movie theater business. The battle between the film industry and the giant Netflix even goaded Dame Helen Mirren to an unregal comment she made in defense of the cinema. Despite many of the films that go straight to rental DVD stores and other heaps of movie shops, it has not discouraged many who aspire to be the next Steven Spielberg. It has not stopped the influx of the crowd that still patronizes movie houses and Helen Mirren's comment that "nothing compares to sitting in a cinema, the incredible moment of relaxation when the lights go down, and the anticipation of being entertained for two hours."

I still go to the movies sometimes at movie houses in malls despite the conveniences afforded by Netflix, Hulu, and Roku plus the Cox selection of films I can choose from. I do not know what made me subscribe to all these outfits even though I very seldom turn them on, except for the vanity of having them all. I watch the film that I think is worth my time and not rely so much on what the reviews of movie critics say. I couldn't care less whether Rex Reed, who used to write reviews on his television show *At the Movies* and was a critic for the *New York Observer*, favorably endorsed a movie. Or the tandem of late Gene Siskel and the erudite Roger Ebert of the *Chicago Sun-Times* suggestion to their readers and viewers that a certain film is worth watching. There are still a hundred or so critics who review films that they think are worth rating one to five stars. While I may not come across many of them and watch what they opine as bad or good, none of them could persuade my wife that the old black-and-white movies or the Technicolor versions of the old films with plenty of spoken dialogue she watches on TCM every late night are better than the raft of box office performances today.

And so do I.

Rivers

Back in the early and mid-sixties, a hundred meters away from what we called a crossing, five kilometers from a village from where I had to walk for four years one way in attending the only high school in town, the Daniel Maramba Bridge spanned the Sinucalan River. The bridge was then very short, less than a third of a mile, and very narrow, with no lanes for pedestrians, so one had to look back and forth for any vehicle that approached the bridge from north to south, going to Dagupan City or coming from Urdaneta as they pass by the town of Santa Barbara. Below the bridge was a strip of the river, where looking down the banks lined by overgrown bamboo trees, women washed clothes and did all of their laundry. The water appeared to be shallow, and in all the years that I walked over the bridge, I never saw fishing as an activity. Potamology was not my suit; I thought of the body of water as more of a stream or a brook, although Sinucalan River was 18.66 kilometers long and was thought to come from Agno River, which originated high up in the Cordillera Mountains and snaked its way into the Lingayen Gulf. I understand that a former president of the country, the second woman to hold the office, who was convicted for graft and election improprieties and was medically confined at a government hospital for what she claims was botched cervical spine surgery, restructured the bridge and brought it up to look wider and modern during her term. Daniel Maramba Bridge, named after the seventh governor of the province, still stands today, though a new highway bypassing the town renders it less busy than it was previously.

The bridge and the river came to mind when I recently I joined a cruise to the Nile River in Egypt. A scheduled trip to see the sights in Egypt we were supposed to join was aborted in 1997 when fifty-eight foreign tourists were held by militants in a Nile Valley attack in Luxor, this coming a few years after wheelchair-borne Leon Klinghoffer was shot and killed on *Achille Lauro* by the Palestinian Liberation Front. For many years, I thought of the river in biblical terms where Nefertiti was known as Queen of the Nile while her husband Akhenaten was pharaoh of Egypt. Though some consider actually the Amazon River as the longest river in the world, there are those who consider the north-flowing river called the Nile in North Africa as the longest, 6,650 kilometers (4,130 miles) flowing through eleven countries and primarily the water source of Egypt and Sudan. The Brazilian scientists who never give up recently suggested after measuring again its length that Amazon River is in fact longer with the new measurements of 6,992 km or 4,345 miles. Ambiguous as comparative lengths of both rivers are, it is well accepted nevertheless that the Amazon is the widest river there is on the planet that there is not a bridge that crosses a river so large that it discharges as much as eight trillion gallons of water each day.

While the Earth's surface is almost covered by water—70.0–71.0 percent—only a small fraction, 2.5 percent, is fresh water, out of the 96.5 percent ocean or saline water. And out of the readily accessible 1.0 percent of fresh water, only 0.3 percent constitutes waters of rivers, swamps, and lakes, according to the US Geological Survey. The rest are thought to be locked in glaciers, polar ice caps, icebergs, and even underground water called groundwater. Though relatively small in terms of the earth's total mass, rivers such as the Nile, Ganges, Amazon, Mississippi, and others have sustained civilization as a source of food, means of navigation and transport for people and goods, drinking, and all sorts of economic, spiritual, and cultural life. Jimmy Houston and the fish that he catches, pats on the head and utters his platitudes before releasing the wiggly critter on his weekly television show is proof enough that these bodies of fresh water are still teeming with aquatic denizens.

Man has the propensity to classify everything that is related to nature. Rivers, with all the characteristics that make each unique and indistinguishable from the rest, are not immune to this human exercise and proclivity. The White Nile and the Blue Nile are named for the two major tributaries of the river. The etymology of a river depends on the language of the ones giving the name. The order of classification also depends on the direction and patterns of its flow or hydrology, whether it ends at some point precipitously or winds its way to the sea, whether it is formed from an iceberg or a glacier high up in the mountains. Occasionally, political boundaries of continents, countries, or empires such as the Danube River, which was once was considered a border of the Roman Empire but is now between Romania and Bulgaria, become a factor in the classification. It is the complexity of rivers and the functions of the environment, the age of the rivers, the chemical composition of its silts and sediments that determine whether it is alluvial or bedrock in its layers, the faults or fractures that make it difficult to come up with a singular river morphology simple enough to understand.

The experience of riding the traditional Nile River sailboat called a *felucca* and the voyage along the River Tosca, seeing the prehistoric ruins preserved for posterity in what was once a complex reserved for queens and pharaohs, was an extraordinary excursion to the past. While Sinucalan River was not as grandiose as it meanders through my old hometown on its way to the mouth of Lingayen Gulf, it nevertheless is a part of a collection that forms a very small Earth treasure called a river.

The Daniel Maramba Bridge is still over it.

Liberty

Diversity

There is a movie recently making the theater circuit and thoroughly reviewed in many news and entertainment magazines called *Crazy Rich Asians*. The reason it is critiqued—and to very good reviews—is that it is the first movie adapted, written by an Asian author, all the characters were all Asians, made it to Hollywood, and released by a major studio and shown nationwide in theaters across the country. While it has been known that the movie industry has shown some foreign-made films, it was generally limited in its scope and distribution and shown only to a few moviegoers in the country, eventually landing in a small screen's heap of collections shown to subscribers who pay a monthly fee. The movie has been bandied as part of an amalgamated effort at making the nation and society culturally diverse. I have read the book and eagerly watched the movie. It was entertaining watching the wretched excesses it depicted of how the rich in Asia behave and the attitude ingrained in their culture. Though it is mostly about Chinese transplants in Singapore, it rings some truth to the old-fashioned tradition of most Asians. I get the feeling that many of those that viewed the film during the showing were aware that such class warfare exists in the Asian community.

It is not only showing this movie this late into what is a tapestry of diversity that as a country needs to clothe itself in. But as the country immerses itself in being called a diverse society, it has to include the many ranges of being diverse. The differences in race, ethnicity, sexual orientation, gender, social class, religion, and ethical values constitute some of the facets of diversity. It also includes political beliefs, national origin, age, or physical abilities. Put these all together and have them melted into a single pot and one comes up with a fabric whose strength, as Stephen Covey says, "lies in its differences not in its similarities."

I came to this country many years ago. I was not under the illusion that I look like majority of the population that inhabited this majestic land of opportunity and unparalleled freedom. I tried to adopt the prevailing customs and traditions and make myself as inconspicuous despite my somatic appearance easily distinguishable by those who were the descendants of Europe and the Western world and who now inhabit and constitute this greatest nation on earth. While I will never be able to change the way I look, I have come to believe that people now after several decades in this country think of me as one of them.

Looking around, however, I found that there are many who have come from foreign lands and settled as well in this country, like me, with the assumption and hope that the present and the future opportunities are much better and more predictable here than where they originally came from. While many have assimilated and incorporated the culture of the West to become citizens of this new land, a few bring in and cling to their prejudices manifested in their behavior, not recognizing the mores of the country they settled in. Retreating to ethnic enclave, not learning the language of the people with whom you find yourself intermingling in society can easily be labeled as not diversity. Inclusion in a society that continually attempts to be diverse results in empowerment, though it is not axiomatic or expected of someone to totally abandon the culture and the practice of where one comes from. The richness of a nation and a society and the engine of growth that comes with it is the diversity of its people. That is why I continue to be part of the ethnic groups that, while adopting and assimilating what this country is made of, have not forgotten where they came from.

In 1993, a special issue of *Time* magazine had on its cover the future of what America would look like. It is an amalgamation of what the

Census Bureau projects that in 2045, the nation will become minority white, with the whites comprising 49.7 percent of the population, 24.6 percent for Hispanics, 13.1 percent for African-Americans, 7.9 percent for Asians, and 3.8 per cent for the multiracial groups. The census projections indicate as well that the post-millennial minorities under eighteen will outnumber the whites in 2020. In a country with a population of 327,339,866, where 83 percent use English as a main language although there is no established law mandating it as an official language of the land, it is always a problem to be as diverse as required.

To appear that it is engaged in this pursuit, there are several ways that the public and private sectors are doing, some of which are well-intentioned and others said to be ill-advised. In the workplace, where diversity has become a buzzword, the human resources department tries to apportion the workforce evenly and fairly to appear considerate of the idea. Some universities base their admissions on the criteria that a certain percentage of their recruits are minorities, or to atone for the past, they have to accept applicants that barely make the grade in lieu of those that deserve to be on the incoming list. Persons running for office and the patronage exhibited by elected politicians are now too common since the days when Emancipation was proclaimed. And if the television is on, there is a noticeable accommodation of other races in the sitcoms and programming that illuminate the ever-expansive screen.

Crazy Rich Asians is long due in coming, in garnering the attention that is emblematic of how the country is marching toward a culture it has to know, see, and appreciate even if it is in a medium called a movie. While it is only an aspect of a society aiming for a multifaceted range of human differences, it is a goal that everyone and every country must strive to achieve. It is called diversity.

> *The worst form of inequality is to try to make unequal things equal.*
>
> *Aristotle*

Plagiarism

I always have this funny idea that somewhere in this wide world, there is always someone that looks and acts and thinks like me. It gives me some comfort to entertain such a thought that in a world populated by billions of human beings, a duplicate of myself, the inherent creativity and talent that I may possess are not wastefully ingrained in one individual. The only concern and fear I have is that in the pursuit of someone who might have committed a malevolent malfeasance, some private eye mistakenly picks me up because I look like that other individual though it might be in a place that I have never been.

I have confirmed, on a number of occasions, that this belief or what you call thesis is true. It has not involved my lookalike but some acquaintance or a friend. I have pointed out to my wife, for instance, as we were walking to an airport a friend's familiar face, only to offer a lame excuse of having mistakenly tapped and greeted him as he passed by. I have also thought of an idea about something that I have on many occasions put in writing to find without any benefit of direct communication that a similar process was entertained by someone somewhere.

Where this became close to home was when one day I was leafing through the pages of the October 2018 issue of the *Smithsonian*, one of the few magazines I found worthwhile subscribing to. In it, I came across an article by William T. Vollmann, all twenty-two pages of it, detailing that "a hundred years ago, the war to end all wars came to a bloody conclusion; a journey along the Western Front that reveals the poignant battle between remembering and forgetting." I read the whole account of how the Germans and the French and the British, the expeditionary American forces, and those involved peripherally during the First World War fought numerous battles and assaults and the many who perished and were buried in graves under rolling hills and skies in Europe. I had never met or heard of Mr. Vollmann until this article. Neither do I know where he resides or where he travels doing research for things that he writes about. I am sure he is an accomplished author and writer. But what got my attention was the article's title, "The End of the Line," which was exactly the title of an editorial I wrote earlier in a surgical magazine that was published and sent to members and friends in late June of 2018. It was a short piece and was about an ethnic organization that, like most organizations in the country, was wracked by declining membership because of attrition, loss of interest, the loss of necessity and purpose of membership, retirement, and voluntary withdrawal and how the remaining members keep the organization's relevance alive.

The chances of somebody accidentally tripping into the circumstances of how the two titles are the same is probably miniscule or nonexistent, like finding a diamond in the rough, considering that the publication I have mine editorialized is limited to members of the organization I belong to, compared to *Smithsonian*, whose circulation and readership is much wider and is sold in every bookstore there is in the country. But it does not give me comfort if someone would think that this is a case of plagiarism although they are separate topics of discussion by two writers separated by familiarity, time, and space. While I retired not too long ago from the profession that I eventually got involved in (I was originally destined to enroll in a seminary because I wanted to be a man of the cloth until Dr. Kildare changed my trajectory), I was involved from then-stenciled years of high school editing and writing to undergraduate and graduate school, where a lanyard hung from my neck with a label announcing I was from the press. It was a rush to be able to have gates and doors opened, covering events that the editor thought worthwhile of a space in the campus newspaper and magazine. I no longer carry the stamp announcing my press affiliation although I have been the editor in chief (a nonpaying job) of this small magazine since the turn of the century. And I must say that in all these years, I have never quoted or copied or paraphrased someone without giving the author credit, memorialized in opening and closing quotes and the sources of information mentioned or appended in reference materials.

Plagiarism, which involves the dishonest and unethical appropriation as one's own of someone's ideas, etched either in speeches, citations, articles, treatises, dissertations or scripts, is patently wrong. One senator and former vice president was forced to withdraw his presidential candidacy in 1988 amid allegations of plagiarism while a student in law school. Other allegations about his declaration of being the first in his family to attend a university as a paraphrase of a British politician's evocation, as well as lifting some passages of speeches of well-known politicians in the country, sank his attempted run as the world's most powerful leader. Plagiarism as a genre is not only a problem relegated to most students ("Plagiarism is the fear of a blank page"—Mokokoma Mokhonoana) and to some writers but sometimes to the most famous personalities. Mention that the charge has been alleged to the present president of Russia when in 2006, he wrote an economic dissertation in which sixteen of the twenty pages were plagiarized from a University of Pittsburgh publication. Or in 2011 when a German defense minister was accused of copiously borrowing from a piece written by someone when he was writing his doctoral dissertation, which was eventually withdrawn by the university after widespread criticism. Or in 2012, a Hungarian president's dissertation was allegedly written similar to a manuscript now at Semmelweis University in Budapest. Even a persistent critic of the present US president, in writing his book, was the subject of many scandals about plagiarizing articles without attributing his sources. A state senator had to withdraw his re-election campaign while a present cabinet secretary "neglected" to give credit to others due for recognition, for information or phrases in his book.

As explosive as the genre is when it erupts, it does not dominate the life of a small fry like me as it does when someone is famous politician, author, or writer. While I can always maintain the purity of not plagiarizing someone's printed idea, an old small-time writer such as I cannot, as a justification, give up this far-fetched thought that somewhere in this wide, wide world there is one that looks and thinks like me. It just so happened that "The End of the Line" crossed Mr. Vollmann and me sans the element of place and time.

If we steal thoughts from the moderns, it will be cried down as plagiarism; if it comes from the ancients, it will be cried up as erudition.

Charles Caleb Colton, English Cleric and Writer

PC (Better Known as Politically Correct)

There is a new addition to everyone's vocabulary these days. It is heard every day, read in every printed material, newspaper or magazine and periodicals on about anything of importance. But it does not seem to be well-defined, making it an indeterminate terminology, the meaning of which depends on who is making it and whose ears it falls on. In the words of a writer attempting to define it in an essay written on the subject matter, it "refers to a matter of inclusive speech, advocacy of non-racist, nonageist, nonsexist terminology, and insistence on affirmative action policies, avoidance of Eurocentrism as reflected on traditional canon of literature, acceptance of multiculturalism as a valued feature of American society, and dismantling hierarchy as controlled by a white male power structure." It is known as PC or otherwise called political correctness. One can only assume that if all of these unabashed intentions were mashed in a single cauldron, we would come up with a recipe that is tasteless to some and tasteful to others. The long and short of that definition, however, is to imply that we should respect all sorts of views in an effort to change all things.

I do not argue with the premise, but looking at it, I found out that has created a polarity among us who have embraced the civility of agreement and disagreement without being disagreeable. True that there are imperfections in our society, now more than ever because of the increased amalgamation of cultures as diverse as the population has become. The framers of the Constitution saw this as a far-ranging and future phenomenon when it allowed with Article V the Congress and several of the states to propose, add, and ratify the twenty-seven amendments presently in the country's Constitution. For many years, *political correctness* was not a hot-button issue. There were some occasions when women were called girls, Asians were Orientals, minorities were slurred, and affirmative actions were not debated as reparations for past inequities. But these orthodoxies, controversial and provocative as they were, silently retreated to the background, the storm they contained was held in abeyance for the sake ostensibly of civility in a society.

The atmosphere has changed. Intentions of not offending anyone have become the norm of people of different persuasions. Insignificant as the comment or beliefs are, the context of what was said or written becomes the apex of what is wrong or right to an ethnic group, culture, or political party and debated ad infinitum. Practices become representative pictures of what is or what is not an affront to somebody else system.

The concept of PC is at times as debilitating as it is constraining. Suddenly it is not right to call the Washington football team Redskins after many years that the name has been in existence. Many wanted to change the name, as it is demeaning to the Indian tribe for which the team was named. It was politically incorrect to have "Chiefs" appended to the Kansas City team, and the controversies would have to be dealt with if the change would be deemed acceptable and palatable. It is changing history as presently taught in schools by toppling the erected statues of those that were originally involved in the struggles they were part of in the past. Many people who oppose affirmative action, preferentially admitting minorities and persons of color as reparations for past transgressions of their ancestors, ahead of those that have better credentials but belong to a fairer race, are afraid to voice their opinion, as it has become politically incorrect to do so. Of course, there are visible and noticeable benefits to the positions espoused by many, such as the prominence attained by those given the chance to advance despite the low status they found themselves in when they were born. It is one of the many societal issues that the so-called establishments, pundits, those who consider themselves experts, and ordinary people like me have to be careful about when we comment or give our pronouncements, which can be construed as politically correct or incorrect.

Sometime back, I found the gravity of being not politically correct. It was one afternoon after the last of the office patients had left when, as I was always inclined to do, I asked my office manager, who was Hispanic, about how her two children were doing in school. "Doing well," she said. Knowing that they were born here but the offspring of immigrants like me and well aware of the fact that if you speak Spanish (one of the five Romance languages as I still remember), you can speak to a quarter of the world's population. I assumed and mentioned casually how great it was that she and her husband were instructing and talking to their two children in Spanish, their native language. She was quiet and her mien changed from a colorful mom to a bland employee. I later found out that her children were not taught or talked to in Spanish at home, and because of their heritage, the children were not automatically mandated or required to memorize the words or phrases and construct sentences derived from their heritage. I did not talk to Lupe anymore about her children, whether they spoke any other language than English. Her sensitivity as to whether she and her husband considered it a parental duty to inculcate the value of the culture they were born in to their two children, or the kids did not consider themselves anything different from those they interact with, did not make it my turf to invade and be correct, in retrospect.

To remain neutral, as if this was a virtue, in the face of the wave of political correctness we are confronted with, I found the truism in an attitude I always assume but forgot to do: not to pass an opportunity to keep my mouth shut.

> *Political correctness is the inability to state certain truths because they may offend certain people.*
>
> *—Dennis Prager, a conservative Jewish radio talk host from New York*

Voting

There is a tree in South Carolina, with layers of bark and moss on its branches as it forms a spread with its 500 years of history. It has weathered all sorts of storms and merciless havoc of Mother Nature. It is the Angel Oak tree at the park of the same name on St. John's Island close to Charleston. It is 66 feet tall, 28 feet wide, and its branches cover a space of 17,200 feet. The tree is the backdrop of William Devane's pitch for a certain gold merchant company, for which he was hired as a spokesman. In this particular commercial, he came into a living room with a plaid shirt, announcing that he would do his two civic responsibilities: what he is telling his audience to do and that is to buy gold, and to exercise his right to vote this coming election cycle. I have not seen William Devane add to his movie and TV filmography since his cameo role in 2014's *Interstellar* or his small-screen appearance in 2015 in the sitcom *Grinder* and in his role in *Jesse Stone: Lost in Paradise*. But he remains effective in his delivery as he has always been in the many films, Broadway shows, and television series he has appeared in. I am not in the market anymore to seek financial stability by storing in my portfolio precious metals that form the vehicle of bartering in ancient era and the standard of currency adopted today by many nations of the world. In the first place, I do not own anything that raises my breathing apparatus above the poverty line. In the second place, I have become contented and satisfied with how to this point I have lived my life.

But what I noted in his line was his mention of his civic duty as a citizen to vote. Whether voting is a right accrued to being a rightful citizen of a country, a civic duty or responsibility, the importance in its exercise and the participation of the citizenry brings the many questions often asked about this prerogative. To this country, it has been a hard-fought century-old campaign and protest led by Elizabeth Cady Stanton, Susan B. Anthony, and Lucy Stone especially for women initially deprived of voicing their opinions in the ballot box, to bring about the 19th Amendment in the US Constitution on August 20, 1920, allowing women to vote. Tennessee became the thirty-sixth state to acquiesce and had the two thirds of the states for Congress to ratify the amendment. Yet it is not a universal prerogative, whether mandatory, right, responsibility, or a duty in a patriarchal society in such countries as Brunei or Saudi Arabia, where women's suffrage is not permitted. Voting, not as simple as it connotes in many countries, denotes many ramifications in governments around the globe. Whether non-citizens are allowed to vote (such as in Portugal or some EU countries), whether it is mandatory (in twenty-two countries including Argentina, Australia, and Belgium), compulsory voting by law (but actually not enforced, as it is in Egypt, Greece, or Gabon), or whether convicted felons are allowed to vote complicate what we generally think is a simple matter. Which states in the US determine which crimes disenfranchise an individual from voting and why are residents of US territories like American Samoa, Puerto Rico, Mariana Islands, Guam, or Virgin Islands, though considered citizens of this country, not allowed to vote in federal elections sometimes can be considered not logical.

I have voted in my district ever since I became eligible to exercise the right as fundamental to my being a citizen of this country. I registered my affiliation to a party that is closest to the beliefs I hold to be true although I do not necessarily endorse—my single vote, which I have always thought counts and matters- the candidate running under the banner I chose. My family is diverse, as there are many political persuasions in the landscape they belong to, bringing us to heated arguments whenever we take the sides of the parties we espouse, at the kitchen table, where most of the discussions wind up. We learned then not to talk about what divides us but, as they say, what unites us.

To make it more a credible and very important right, I ran for an elected office in a college district for twenty years unopposed, with four years of an unexpired six-year term before I gave up the toga and the gown that comes along with yearly commencement/graduation exercise. While I consider voting a right and a privilege, I also see it as a responsibility of choosing a government that shapes the society I continue to live in. Despite the imperfections, alleged manipulations, and accusations, it is still the best alternative to a system that does not afford this hard-fought freedom.

William Devane has not convinced me about his gold. But surely, he moved my derriere to go out and vote.

> *Always vote for principle, though you may vote alone, you may cherish the sweetest reflection that your vote is never lost.*
>
> *John Quincy Adams, sixth US president*

Drugged

One morning a year ago, the world was astounded with the news that one of the music legends of the century was found dead at his Paisley studio in Minneapolis. Prince, as he was known, was only fifty-seven and over the ensuing weeks when the results of toxicology were finally revealed, he was found to have died from an overdose of fentanyl, a very potent painkiller that is only obtained with a prescription from a licensed physician. How he was able to obtain it without a prescription remains a speculation, although the conjecture was that it was given by a friend or an associate.

The talented Philip Seymour Hoffman, at forty-six, overdosed on February 2, 2014, from a mixture of heroin, cocaine, benzodiazepines, and amphetamines. Add to this mix Robin Williams, Whitney Houston, Heath Ledger, Michael Jackson, Anna Nicole Smith, and countless celebrities, and we are all drawn to and reminded that the current opioid epidemic is the worst drug crisis in American history. Though the deaths of these celebrities bring attention to the addiction to a segment of the population, they do not totally represent the ripples of death in small stores, the stretches of highways in small towns, in the surrounding suburbia, in rural Appalachia and the coal towns, where generally there is only one licensed physician prescribing pain medications.

The death rates from overdoses from rural areas now outpace the rate from larger metropolitan areas, which historically had higher rates. A majority of the drug overdose deaths, six out of ten, involve opioids. This includes opioid prescription such as oxycodone, hydrocodone, and methadone, which since 1990 together with heroin has quadrupled. Ninety-one Americans die every day from opioid overdose, and from 2000 to 2015, more than half a million people died from drug overdose, including eighteen women who die every day as well. In 2015 alone, 33,000 people died from overdose, nearly equal to the number of deaths from car crashes. Deaths from heroin alone surpassed gun homicides in that particular year. The list of drugs abused includes not only opioids but also tranquilizers/sedatives and methamphetamines, over-the-counter cough and cold medicines, mescaline, cannabis or marijuana in some states that have legalized their recreational uses.

Prescription Drug Abuse

Drug abuse is a serious public health problem that affects many Americans. It is the leading cause of injury death in the United States. Between 1999 and 2013, the death rate involving prescription opioids has increased four times, accompanied by quadrupling of prescribing rates during the same fifteen-year period.

Although most people take their medications responsibly, 52 million used prescription drugs for nonmedical reasons at least once in their lifetimes. Almost one in twenty adolescents and adults—20 million people—used prescription when it was not prescribed for them. They get it free from a friend or relative. However, those who are at risk of overdose get them in ways that are different from those who use them less frequently. People get their own opioids using their own prescription (27 percent), from friends or relatives for free (26 percent) or buying from them (23 percent), or buying from a drug dealer (15 percent), with the latter increasing the risk of overdose four times more likely than the average user. The increase in heroin and heroin overdose has tripled over the same period of time. Seventy-five percent of heroin users started their heroin use with prescription opioids in the early '60s when it was associated with the fact that it was less expensive and easier to produce than some prescription opioids. Most of the heroin comes from Mexico. It has been shown that deaths from heroin overdose affect both genders, all age groups, all geographic regions, and all ethnicities.

Prescription and Drugs

While many believe that drugs are not dangerous because they are prescribed by a doctor, it is often that abuse of the same leads to dependence. The recent explosion and abuse of opioids as well as the emerging class of street drugs called synthetic cannabinoids have been, to some extent, due to the oversupply of prescription drugs by physicians for the treatment or management of pain, purportedly for trauma, surgery, or chronic pain in non-cancer patients. While these drugs play an important role in managing some types of pain, there are many health providers who are overprescribing these drugs. Among specialists managing acute and chronic pain, prescribing rates are highest among pain medicine specialists (49 percent) surgery (37 percent), physical medicine/rehabilitation (36 percent). However, primary care providers account for half of the opioid pain relievers dispensed. Although prescription opioids help manage some types of pain, there is not enough evidence that they improve chronic pain function and quality of life. There has not been an overall change in the amount of pain reported among Americans, but the supply of prescription opioids remains high, with one out of five patients with non-cancer pain or pain-related diagnoses in many office-based sting operations conducted. It has been said that many organizations, like the American Pain Society, the Joint Commission, Veterans Health Administration, make treatment of pain a priority with little or no regard to the complications of overdose or abuse of the drugs. There has been a little movement though to address this problem now that it has become an epidemic.

Hydrocodone is the most commonly misused prescription opioid, but oxycodone and methadone are most commonly implicated in fatal overdose. Complications and side effects include as well bradycardia, hypotension, and respiratory depression. In addition, other health issues such as chronic constipation, fall among the elderly, neonatal abstinence syndromes from women abusing opioids, and transition to IV opioids remain. These result in significant ER visits and subsequent inpatient hospitalizations, with over $50 billion cost of health care for this group of the population.

Who Is Most Affected

Prescription opioids vary according to gender, age, and ethnicity.
- Homeless youths are more likely to use illegal drugs and alcohol than most.
- The death rates and complications tend to be higher in non-Hispanic whites, Native Americans, and those that came from lower socioeconomic status. Non-Hispanic whites are more likely to use prescription opioids than Hispanics. There are no significant differences in prescription opioid use between non-Hispanic whites and non-Hispanic blacks.
- People living in rural areas (clusters in the Southeast) especially in the Appalachian region
- People who obtained multiple prescriptions of controlled substances, especially combinations of opioid analgesics and benzodiazepines from multiple providers
- People who take high daily dosages of opioid pain relievers
- Men, although women are more likely to use prescription opioids

Cannabis and Cannabinoids

In the United States, the national support (93 percent) for the use of cannabis, both medical and medicinal, has added to the drug problem. The total number of states with some form of legal pot use is twenty-four; however, recreational marijuana is now fully legal in states like Alaska, Colorado, Nevada, Oregon, Washington, California, Massachusetts, and the District of Columbia. Considerable variation exists from state to state in the medical use of cannabis, including how it is produced, distributed, consumed, and the medical condition for which it is used.

The first state to pass an effective cannabis law was California in 1996. Several states followed the initiative, and Hawaii in 2000 became the first state to legalize marijuana by the state legislature. Subsequently, recreational use was placed into the ballot referendum in other states for tax and financial advantages for the state's coffers. The exorbitant cost of incarceration for drug offenses involving marijuana was also one of the factors these states decriminalized cannabis use. While present studies so far have not seen a rash of overdose from the recreational use of marijuana, the incidence of psychoactive effects have been on the rise.

At the federal level, cannabis remains a prohibited substance. Under the Controlled Substances Act of 1970, the Drug Enforcement Agency classifies cannabis as a Schedule I drug. Of late, however, the Justice Department has not actively enforced the prohibitive policy of the law in states that have approved the initiative. The Rohrabacher-Farr amendment signed into law December 2014 prohibited the Justice Department from spending funds to interfere in state medical cannabis laws. The Justice Department has also refrained from enforcing federal laws against the use of recreational cannabis.

Synthetic cannabinoids, known as K2 or Spice on the streets, are gaining popularity. These are sold at convenience stores, drug paraphernalia shops, and on the Internet as air fresheners with a "not for human consumption" label. This allows these drugs to escape scrutiny. With its euphoric effects, visual hallucinations, paranoid delusions, suicidal ideations, vomiting, drowsiness, chest pains, dizziness, and a host of somatic and psychological symptoms, synthetic mimics the natural cannabis and its unpredictable effects.

Present Response to the Epidemic

The federal government, cognizant of the ongoing opioid problem, launched several initiatives and efforts for both the public and private sectors to address the present epidemic. Former President Obama issued several directives to HHS, FDA, and other agencies such as the Department of Veteran Affairs and the Department of Defense, identifying opportunities and other additional collaborative activities between the government, state and local stakeholders. The federal government proposed $1.1 billion in new funding to address the prescription opioid and heroin abuse and released $94 million to health care centers in forty-five states under the Affordable Care Act to improve and expand delivery of substance abuse services in health centers, with specific focus on the treatment of opioid disorders in underserved areas. One of the three-pronged attacks directed by the former administration requires the HHS Assistant Secretary for Planning and Development and Evaluation (ASPE) for the expanded use and distribution of naloxone, an antagonist for opioids. The drug eases withdrawal symptoms and minimizes cravings for opioids.

What is more effective and appears to be working in combating the epidemic is the promise of prescription drug monitoring (PDMP) passed by forty-nine states, limiting the number that can be prescribed for opioids, the practitioner limited to a seven-day supply of opioids for acute pain at a given time. It also monitors patient who "doctor shop" and that all controlled substances be written electronically. Pills that might be stolen, sold, or given to a friend or relative without doctor supervision would hopefully diminish or prevented.

As to the present administration, aside from the Interdict Act signed by President Trump, the directives to appropriate agencies and pronouncements of addiction as a national public health emergency, not being society's future, the seriousness of the $6 billion passed in the Senate and signed in a budget deal for fiscal years 2018 and 2019 for combating the drug crisis, 115 people still die every single day.

With all the steps presently undertaken by the federal, state, and local governments, and several public and private entities to combat this ongoing epidemic, it is still hard to know all the fronts and where to begin if we ever solve or outrun the problem.

The other day, I was rummaging through my practice files when I came to the old triplicate prescription forms I was issued the very first time I started my surgical practice in the mid-seventies by the Medical Board and the Department of Public Safety, for me to use in writing a controlled substance. More than half of the 300 prescription blanks were not used in the thirteen thousand, eight hundred seventy days I wore the white gown or the scrubs, which I still wear once in a while when I go to surgical missions in Third World countries. I have not given them up as is required when you hang up your gloves, because despite closing up the shop, I still renew biennially all my licenses and permits. I suppose the remaining numbers of unused forms would not change because I would not like being one of the many who contributes to the raging epidemic.

> (Reprinted and adapted from the *Philippine Surgeon* magazine, July 2017)

> *But I will say that the drugs are much more ferocious than they used to be. There are people wrecking their lives with addiction, which seems much more severe.*
>
> —*Armistead Maupin, an American writer*

Political Parties

It is a well-known fact that one individual alone cannot change a system, an idea, a policy, or a structure. It needs a collective group, and when people or groups of people of similar persuasion, ideas, opinions, and interests organize together and influence or achieve control of the society they live in, a political party is born. Those that constitute a political party, its members, and affiliates bind together and persuade others to join then in an effort to inform and stimulate them and nominate candidates who can implement their ideas. In the United States, the first political party was called the Federalists, put together in 1787 by Alexander Hamilton and opposed in 1796 by Thomas Jefferson, who did not believe in a strong central government. Today, as recently as the nomination to the Supreme Court of the now Justice Kavanaugh to the vacant post of the retiring Justice Anthony Kennedy, was as contentious as the accusations against the then-prospective nominee, as is his nomination by members of the Federalist Society.

One cannot underestimate the role political parties play in spreading their ideologies to the citizens of their country, where the political system embraces a one-party, a two-party, or multiparty system. Political parties are the essence of any government, and they define and influence the direction of what the leaders—or politicians as they are most commonly called—generally take as representatives of their constituents. While political systems are often complex, it is the interest of a nation, I would like to believe, that drives their existence. It is the political parties that help people formulate their opinions on issues that are brought and debated before them as to the merits and demerits of the subject. It is about the views and the platforms that are communicated in a free society, that the public is educated and the exchange of ideas is fostered.

There are disadvantages to having political parties that the phenomenon is not all complex to comprehend at times. Belonging to and affiliating with a political party and its groupthink makes the followers blind, lose their independence, become selfish and narrow-minded in their way of thinking. Political parties also create, however much it becomes a serious show of political awareness, that the party they belong to is more important than the interest of the state, disrupting national unity, defining people into whether they belong to the right or left of the spectrum. It often results in violent clashes when political parties and their adherents belittle the other party or a deadlock on government functions when parties don't agree on certain policies or issues.

In the United States, the modern political party system is dominated by the Democratic Party and the Republican Party. These two parties have won every US presidential election since 1852 in a winner-take-all system, as there is no reward for a second-place finish. The plurality has been a disadvantage to the smaller and several third parties that sprouted in the past to challenge the system. The Democratic Party, which was founded in 1828 by Andrew Jackson, is the oldest active political party in the world. Thomas Jefferson laid the heritage of its founding when in May 12, 1792, together with some of his cohorts, he opposed the principles of the Federalist Society. The modern-day Democratic Party supports more government spending on social services, less on military spending, reducing economic inequality and that the wealthiest Americans pay the highest amount in taxes. The Republican Party was founded on March 20, 1854, by former Whigs who were antislavery in the South; it was thought to be formally formed with the nomination of Abraham Lincoln to the presidency in 1860 in Chicago. It is more conservative on issues and believes that the federal government should stay away from playing a big role in people's lives, lower taxes and less government spending on social programs and less intrusion and intervention in business and economic activity of its citizens. The surprise election in 2016 of Donald Trump to the US presidency has brought animosity and distrust among the followers and adherents of the political parties despite the claims of positive changes brought about by the new administration. In a polarized society, the chaos and the confrontation created, however, do not mitigate the net results of having a political party system that the world admits as being the freest in the universe.

The role and the merits of having political parties that people can be affiliated with because of having the same or similar ideas, aims, and opinions do not necessarily happen or translate in other countries like in the United States. Think of some countries in Africa, where the politicians in power with their monolithic party system grip the population presented with a token ineffectual two-party or multiparty choice during election time. Or some so-called democratic republics' political operatives squeeze the daylights of someone who belongs to another political party and has the courage and wherewithal to stand up against them during election time. Holding and perpetuation of power as basic as human ego has always been, is one of the strongest motivations for some to sweep away the expediency of having political parties, which is the lifeblood of a democratic institution.

Ever since I was declared to be eligible to vote, I registered to be a member of a party whose values are similar to or close to what I believe in. I have never missed any primary or a general election when the time comes. But I have not always voted for the candidate of the party when he or she stands for what I think is in contravention to my principles and ideas. I have made it a point that belonging to a particular party should not hamper my own individuality and should not drive me blindfolded to the gallows. Does this actually make me an independent? My family belongs to different political persuasions. I know of these as one day, I was surprised to see a picture of one of my granddaughters holding a sticker of another candidate whom obviously her parents were supporting. Some admitted the party they belong to and which candidates they favor. My sister-in-law has removed from her will those relatives who declared themselves opposite to what political party she belongs to. Our kitchen political discussions have been reduced to a minimum in an effort to diminish heated rhetoric about what is best for the country.

It is a free country. And common sense still is best, though these days, even it does not seem to be as common as we want it to be.

> *There is nothing which I dread so much as a division of the republic into two great parties, each arranged under its leader, and concerting measures in opposition to each other. This, in my humble apprehension, is to be dreaded as the greatest political evil under our Constitution.*
>
> *John Adams, letter to Jonathan Jackson, October 2, 1789*
>
> *Let us not seek the Republican answer or the Democratic answer, but the right answer. Let us not seek to fix the blame for the past. Let us accept our responsibility for the future.*
>
> *John F. Kennedy*

Health Care

Healthcare in the United States is a hotly contested issue that consumes the public and the different stakeholders in the debate. When the Affordable Care Act was introduced and the provisions it entailed were approved after acrimonious passage in Congress, the effects on all, especially on us, the medical providers of health care, were explained in all the forums I attended at that time. It remained confusing to me as ever, and though it was eventually the law of the land, there were still many questions unanswered, which to someone like me demanded commonsense answers, aware that this age-old problem can't have all the solutions acceptable to the more than 300 million people in this country. Questions include why a consumer of health care cannot purchase a policy thought to be reasonable and cheaper from a company that does not cross a state line, or a young healthy individual subsidizing someone else's medical problem by paying a higher premium than he or she is supposed to. Ultimately, the question redounds to whether health care is a right or an entitlement of a person in a democratic society. One provision of the Act that I especially favor is that persons with pre-existing conditions cannot be denied coverage by those that insure the health of the policy owners. It remains today a bone of contention that both political parties say they will retain in its original form despite the attempt at "repeal and replace" efforts by the new administration.

As the issue is controversial even up to the present, the many facets of the problem that everyone faces remains complex, the utopian model and its implementation continues to be elusive, the welfare of those involved and the economics of equitable distribution of resources continues to stump health organizations and policy makers. I can only present the side of the health care provider—as the new paradigm shift calls doctors nowadays—going through a period of what was called then the golden age of medicine to what the profession now has to face. The United States has a highly developed health care system available to all regardless of whether one has the capacity to pay or not. One of the problems that a health care provider has to deal with is the patient that goes to the emergency room for non-emergency condition simply because the individual does not have any health insurance. The health care provider on call leaves his or her office when called to attend to someone who shows up at the emergency department because by law, he or she is not allowed to turn the patient down. The hospital then cost-shifts to the paying customers, who for most part unknowingly are charged to recoup the hospital's expenses for the nonpaying patient. Every year, the government issues a list of the current procedure and international disease codes to every physician that details how much it is going to pay if one accepts participating or not in this cost-benefit analysis. The payment system has become a blueprint for all insurers as to how much they reimburse their enrollees based on the government's economy-of-scale model. While it has been mentioned that in a country such as the United States has 44 million uninsured and 38 million with inadequate health insurance even before the Affordable Care Act was passed, there never was a time when a patient was denied medical service because of lack of insurance.

The continuum of health care has grown to involve many aspects of its delivery system. These are continually addressed by health plans, physicians, clinics and hospitals, consumers and other health care professionals. The era of horse-and-buggy days and doctors making house calls, accepting payment in kind from patients they serve is long gone. Fee-for-service, once the norm of a doctor's practice, has been abolished by economists and sociologists, replaced with current procedural terminology and disease codes assigned monetary values in whatever part of the country you live and where you practice your craft. Disease for which someone is hospitalized is limited by the length of stay (LOS) regardless of age or co-morbidities, and given a price for the duration, diagnostic modalities, and the treatment administered. Whatever is not expended is considered a profit for the facility. One can easily determine from the facts the necessity of creating risk managers by the hospitals to remind doctors of where they are with every hospital admission. Insurance companies covering different jurisdictions in the country created as well risk management inspectors to go over the financial records of doctors when the companies suspect any billing wrongdoings and are paid on commission on what they recover. To make it more user and patient friendly, the ACA mandated the health care providers to incrementally use electronic medical record system with every patient encounter to make it more accessible to other providers and for health payers to reimburse providers shortly after providing the service if the submission of claims is complete. Gaming this system has been anathema to the implementation of the system, both of the use of electronic medical systems, which sprouted many software companies that defeated the original intent of accessibility and the cost the practitioner has to bear because of the non-funded mandate the new law imposes. The insurers have also gone around the concept of shorter time payment scheme by demanding from the provider some more data about their subscriber that has received medical service. There are benefits, however, to some of these new provisions, but most are offset by the disadvantages experienced by providers and consumers alike.

If the purpose of the ongoing health care problems and its solutions to date has been to wrestle with the increasing longevity of its senior citizens, the cost of providing health care to all and its economic impact on the national budget projected to be 28 percent in 2028, the search for the fix is far from over. It is true that spending for health care is a staggering $8,600–$8,700 per capita in the United States, with Norway coming in close second. Last year's expenditure amounting to nearly $3.7 trillion is 25 percent of the government's gross domestic product. While the objective of the government health delivery system that all its citizens receive services, when needed at a cost-effective rate, is ideal and commendable, the concept of a single-payer system is variously looked upon by several proponents to enable a more equitable and judicious use of resources. Preventive medicine, the use of physician extenders staffing now urgent care centers instead of physicians have become a substitute for unnecessary emergency room visits. The fact remains, however, that the United States still remains a mecca of the best health care delivery system in the world despite its continuing quest for integration, imperfect market conditions, several players in the balance of power, and the costly unequal outcomes that sometimes a technology-driven economy brings.

In my days as a medical student and the postgraduate education I undertook and the continuing medical education required to keep my license up to date, the business of running an office was and is not offered as part of a curriculum. One has to learn de novo all the permutations of how much to charge to cover one's overhead, how to allocate limited resources to improve and upgrade the appurtenances of an office practice, and how much continuing education one needs to invest not only to keep up with what is new and continually happening in one's field but to be able give the best to the patients that enter your doorsteps. Today's health care delivery is a far cry from the answer you give when someone at a medical school interview asks what motivates you to become a doctor. You answer, of course, your humanitarian desire to be of help alleviate the physical suffering of humanity. While this may lead to the acceptance of wearing the white coat of becoming someday a medical professional, the motivation loses its operative meaning in this present environment eventually.

There are still many though that believe that health care is a calling that renews not only the body but the soul as well. That is one reason that drives someone like me to go to Third World countries and join surgical missions where one forgets about the economics of a medical practice and remembers to concentrate on a delivery of health care to an underserved but appreciative patient.

Fixing health care and fixing the economy are two sides of the same coin.

Anonymous

America enjoys the best health care in the world, but the best is no good if folks can't afford it and doctors can't provide it.

Bill Frist, MD, cardiovascular and lung transplant surgeon, former senator and majority leader of the US Senate

Term Limits

Now that the midterm elections are over, what term limits stand for would not be considered a political utilitarian talk. It is, as every voter knows, a legal restriction to curb the potential for monopoly, intended for those seeking elected office. It has a long history imposed by two ancient republics in the early years, Athens and Rome, to restrict political dynasties by limiting the terms specific to the position or office to which an individual may serve, subject to the will of the electorate. In the United States, because of the 22nd Amendment to the Constitution in 1951, the president is limited to two terms, the vice president with no term limits, as with the Representatives to the House and the Senators to the Senate. Franklin Delano Roosevelt was the only president elected for four terms, and this was before the 22nd Amendment was ratified. While there have been several attempts to place limits on running for those offices, most fail because an office holder can be swept out of office or retained to continue representing the interest of the people by the biennial elections, a better substitute for term limits. Various states of the union have state laws that regulate the terms of governors and state legislators as well as some officials. If anything, some elected officials voluntarily retire from the position they hold, sometimes for several decades, for career change, returning to a more lucrative private sector job, or some suddenly find that spending more time with their family is an important prerogative in their lives. Others consider the present position they are in as a stepping stone to another office they aspire to. Some eventually step down because of the divisive political environment they find themselves in. For a good politician, limiting his or her term is considered short; for another that is discovered to be bad, it becomes too long to wait to shoo him or her out.

The ancient Chinese philosopher Lao Tzu said, "A leader is best when people barely know when he exists, when his work is done, his aim fulfilled, they will say: we did it ourselves." Today, however, one has to be known for what spoils one might bring to the people one represents. If not, the next time one stands in supplication for another chance to serve or represent their interests, one might be turned down. Those that taste power find later that it always is intoxicating and will continue to perpetuate its sensual effects by purposely forgetting its limits. I recall many years ago when a neophyte politician was running for Congress in his district, promising everyone that he would only stay if elected for two terms. He was elected by his constituents though he belonged to a minority party, on the strength of his promise. After three terms, he was reminded by his opponent and the electorate of his earlier promise and was voted down. But during his incumbency, while ably representing the needs of his district, he wielded whatever influence he had in the interest of his family and himself.

The expected change in the composition of the Lower House brought about by the results of the recently concluded elections demonstrate not only the many factors that influence the people at a given period but also the mood and beliefs about prevailing issues that dominate the scene. These are generally prioritized by competing biases, interests, parties, groups, and individuals through speeches, rhetorical ideas bought by funds raised by those espousing the sides of the aisle. The change always determines the direction the country or the society will follow, whether a new focus on what presently prevails is advanced or continued, or whether a new path will be pursued. In more than two and one half centuries since the country's founding, however, the change in the direction has never been a permanent government fixture.

Term limits can be consecutive or lifetime, the latter more restrictive. With lifetime, once the office holder has served up to the limit, he or she may not run for election to the office again. While this could be for six years, modifications have sometimes been made to the definition. Consecutive limits the office holder to serve in a particular office usually after one term, but after a set period of time, he or she may run for the original office again. In different countries around the globe, term limits are defined by whether the country is a presidential republic, such as those in South America, or operates under a parliamentary system of government like the United Kingdom, which is less likely to impose term limits for as long as the parliament has confidence in its chosen leaders. The presidents of South American countries are generally limited to a single six-year term, making a presidential election, for instance, in Mexico a non-incumbent political contest. Since the breakup of the USSR into the Russian Federation, the head of state—the president of the country— can serve more than two terms, provided these are not consecutive. The federation's present president favors that term limits be removed. Of course, in a country where a citizenry is governed by a dictator whose yoke is imposed and implemented by a subservient military, the limits of term in holding an office are nonexistent.

Understanding term limits has not been so complicated in a society where positions are well clarified by a living document called the Constitution. It is the wisdom of those who framed this document with the idea of preventing entrenched interests staying permanently holding power that has remained stable and unchanged throughout several centuries of its existence. While the modern-day government is believed to be dysfunctional and at times corrupt, the usefulness of having term limits remains fundamentally necessary for a functioning democracy. It is one reason that I like living in a system where I might not favor someone like a president of my country or a governor in my state who is chosen by the people to lead but know that after his or her term expires, he or she can no longer run again. And for those office-seekers who are immune to this limitation, I as well as the people eligible to vote can impose our brand of term limits through the ballot box.

> *Whenever a man casts a longing eye on offices, a rottenness begins in his conduct.*
>
> *Thomas Jefferson, American diplomat, lawyer and the third president of the United States*
>
> *After a time, civil servants tend to become no longer servants and no longer civil.*
>
> *Winston Churchill, former British prime minister*

Taxes

It is hard getting used to being on the other side of the fence. A momentary loss of identity from being a doctor to a patient requires a drastic change in attitude if only for a temporary loss of self-esteem and hierarchy. But as one approaches the end of a yardstick in life, this role reversal becomes real and inevitable as the two things in life that are certain and bound to come: death and taxes. A few weeks ago, I called a doctor's office for an appointment, and in a sweet voice, the lady at the appointment desk gave me a date that my wife was to see the doctor. It was for December 7. Nonchalantly, I asked, out of curiosity, if the date December 7 was historically significant to her. Either she was too young to know or remember or she was not in an attentive mode during her history lesson days, but she said no—it was just another day in the office. Parenthetically, I mentioned that it was a day of infamy when Pearl Harbor was attacked surreptitiously and was the beginning of the United States involvement in World War II in the Far East. It is not a day that many people remember as it draws farther and farther away from the memory books. But mention April 15, and majority, if not all, are constantly reminded of the last day our federal government needs those forms called tax returns enclosed and pledged checks to keep its machinery going.

Our government relies predominantly on funding its operation from an enforced contribution, essentially a bill and not a voluntary donation or payment from its citizens. The tax structure that the government has developed is complicated in a market economy where policies such as the level of taxation, the amount of taxes and how the revenue should be raised, the different types of taxations such as capital tax, individual, and income tax are so hard to comprehend and understand that 70 to 75 percent of us require a professional tax preparer to avoid being penalized for the confusion the obligation brings. While the origin and the concepts of taxation from the very beginning have been to provide the goods and the services of the community, it has engendered some transparency problems through inevitable shortcomings, loopholes, and perceived inequality to some segments of society and distribution of resources. The power of the US Congress to collect the income tax was not until the 16th Amendment was ratified in 1913, when the threat of another expensive war loomed on the horizon. In a democratic society such as ours, the institutions of our government are continually looking for ways to make the imposition equitable, although the consensus of how to achieve this nirvana becomes a contentious proposition depending on who controls the levers of power. The taxes are collected annually by the Internal Revenue Service, the income tax constituting more than 50 percent of the federal government's revenue. The income tax is considered progressive tax, dependent upon the earnings, salaries, and profits of the individual. While the income tax rates are not immutably fixed as they depend on economic changes and indices, there is a percentage of the population who are exempted from filing this annual government-imposed obligation. Those are part of the population whose adjusted gross income falls below the taxable limits imposed by the government.

With the increasing population, the diverse ethnicity, and the subsidies and entitlements the government has to confront, together with the leaders' and authorities' penchant for delivering what is thought to be for the public good, it is not surprising that over the past few years, what the government collects from its citizens does not satisfy what it spends for the services it provides. Consequently, it borrows money from others, creating a debt, a budget deficit, the interest payment crippling the government machinery in the years to come, supposedly falling into the laps of the incoming generation.

The problem has developed to an economic crisis, but mostly the solution offered has been to tighten the government's belt and to live within its means. This sustainable solution has remained illusory so far, as the government's priority is to continue subsidizing its ever-increasing programs and entitlements. As far as I know, the trend to arrest and put an end to this financial skullduggery remains a mirage.

Ever since I moved to this country almost half a century ago, I have always filed my income taxes, starting with a small tax preparer in New York, up to the time I moved to Texas, and now in Nevada. I have kept the tax returns, and in the professional years of practice, the returns have been voluminous. I found out that this type of document hoarding—which I assumed I took from my father—helped me later on in determining the social security payments I was entitled to. In some years, I found that I had an unexpected refund from our government, which always makes my day. On others, I have to write and enclose a check that my tax preparer said was due. While most taxpayers give the IRS what it is due, I, like most everyone else, always make sure that every penny of my assessable income is what it is after all the allowable itemized deductions are accounted for. The tax structure and how much taxes one has to pay do not seem to be a question to many but for the collective cost of how the government spends and overspends for many of the services it provides. I do not protest or voice any opposition to my tax, however small compared to some, except when I learn that the government buys a toilet seat for more than a thousand dollars or pays out excessive expenditure on some bureaucrat's trip to some foreign country, ostensibly for a fact-finding mission that could easily be accessed by local information and investigation.

I recently started collecting and collating last year's receipts for this year's tax return. It is what I do before April 15. With the new tax laws supposedly made simpler and the choice of deductions reduced to whether taking the increased standard tax deduction or itemizing what is allowable if the sum is more than the standard deduction, it is not an immediate decision I have to make before the last day of filing. But I will meet the deadline, maybe long before the due date.

I just hope the government will wisely spend the money collected from its citizens like me.

> *The problem is not that the people are taxed too little. The problem is that the government spends too much.*
>
> *Ronald Reagan, thirty-third governor of California and fortieth president of the United States*
>
> *I am proud to pay taxes in the United States; the only thing is, I could be just as proud for half the money.*
>
> *Arthur Godfrey, radio and TV personality, Radio Hall of Fame awardee*

Crime

While it is not universally accepted that the phrase "Lies, damned lies, and statistics" are attributed to the late British prime minister Benjamin Disraeli, as it never was in his works; nevertheless, it has been quoted many times over when it bolsters an argument or casts doubt and aspersion on an opponent's point of view. The phrase has at times been attributed to many prominent and political persons at that time, but it was Mark Twain who brought and popularized the saying in the United States and at other times was erroneously thought to be the originator of the phrase. Later he said, "Figures often beguile me," when he wrote and published his autobiography in the *North American Review* way back in 1906. As recently as few years ago, the National Institutes of Health challenged the veracity of a peer-reviewed article in a prestigious journal when it found out that the statistics quoted skewed the authors' justification of their preconceived conclusion.

There is, however, a statistic that is issued every year by law enforcement that is accepted verbatim. It is the statistic on crime, which is defined as an action, either an offense or omission, defying the state or country laws and punishable as a felony or, if considered minor infraction, a misdemeanor. It is a problem not only in the United States but also around the world. It occurs in different forms, such as violent crimes exemplified by murder, robbery, assaults, and rape. It can include burglary and theft, considered property crimes. Gambling, drug abuse, and prostitution, classified victimless crimes, recently became a sensational topic for the media when a cause celebre got ensnared having sex in a massage parlor in Florida prior to his team's win over the Kansas City Chiefs. And with the advent of new technology, scams, intellectual and identity thefts have spawned a different breed of criminals and crime that law enforcement agencies are trying to catch up with. While society believes that crime cannot be totally eradicated from its midst, it believes that those responsible need to be punished for their transgression.

Crime is a social problem. The causes are myriad, variously attributed to lack of respect, lack of responsibility, poverty, low self-esteem, parental inadequacy, abuse, family violence, or lack of communication. While it affects almost every family to some greater or lesser degree, the fact is the yearly survey of crime statistics by an institution such as the Federal Bureau of Investigation and the compilation it gathers from the law enforcement agencies across the country indicate that local and unique conditions factor into the report. There are many variables that affect what and how crime is committed in a particular town, city, state, or region in the country. Think of the city of Chicago, where murder rates are on the rise, 660 last year alone, especially among the poor and disenfranchised on the south side of town. Despite the several preventive and reduction mechanisms the police department and the city say they brought to combat the lawlessness, it remains on an upward trend. The UCR (Uniform Crime Reporting) program that FBI has developed in conjunction with law enforcement agencies gives access to the public about statistical analysis of crime in the United States. While the report on 2017 indicates that after the previous two years of consecutive increase, there is a decline of violent crimes by 0.2 percent and property crimes dropping to 3.0 percent in 2016, it really does nothing to allay the fears of the population, 55% of Americans who say that crime still is a very serious concern. Neither does the statistic that violent crimes such as robbery, murder, rape, and assaults happen still every 24 seconds every day and that in 2017, there were still 1,247,321 reported violent crimes. And this does not include other offenses such as thefts and arson.

Winston Churchill famously said, "Statistics are like a drunk on a lamppost: more support than illumination." It is true that it pays to be aware of how the conditions in a society are influencing the commission of the crime, and if it can be approached with solutions or rehabilitations, statistics can be both a support and illumination. But for every step society takes to face up to the "drunk" situation, another aspect of crime emerges. Cybercrime is a relatively new phenomenon causing more problems for our law enforcement agencies and bringing concern and grief to victims. I am even surprised at the audacity of Def Con, one of the world's largest hacker groups, holding their convention in same city of Las Vegas a week after an association of technology innovators on how to improve or institute upgrades in the daily lives of potential customers. While it is true that the convention is attended by some government employees, security researchers, and many more, it is generally a hackers' meet where the attendees have a general interest in software, computer data, phone, chip architecture, lock-picking, digitalized codes and how these can be modified or hacked. In one segment of a newscast describing the convention, one hacker proudly stated that the newer vehicles have many computer chips in them that a hacker using an alias or a handle (participants do not use real identities, especially during conventions) can intercept and make the vehicle stop, cross a lane, ignore the engine switch, and have these operative until the owner pays a fee to have the cracks restored. By the way, 22,000 attended the hackers' convention in 2016.

It worries me that even though the 2017 statistics and the preliminary 2018 report released by the FBI showed a decline in the national crime rate, staggering national UCR data of 382.9 violent offenses, or 2,362 property crimes per 100,000 of the local population, reinforces the belief that at some point in somebody's life, he or she can be a victim of crime. Lately, I have been in the market looking around for security systems where, at the touch of a button on my portable phone or device, I can visualize someone attempting to burglarize or commit crime in my house. Though I already have installed a security system, it is not of the closed circuit television variety, many models of which are offered today. Neither do Mr. Wesson and Mr. Smith, as recommended by a locksmith I hired one day, prevent a determined criminal from carrying out his or her deed. I have not settled on which security or alarm systems I would install additionally in my house. But whatever it is, I hope that statistics, this time on crime, would not turn out to be a damned lie.

Doctors

Hippocrates was a Greek physician, the author of the Hippocratic Oath, which up to now is recited by newly minted physicians after four years of passage from medical schools. The journey starts with donning a short white coat on an exciting, momentous day celebrated with a white coat ceremony observed today by more than 100 medical schools marking the start of a medical career. The oath expresses ethical principle of confidentiality and non-maleficence articulated in the phrase "first do no harm." Though breaking the oath results in no direct punishment, it is arguably considered, in modern parlance, medical malpractice, which courts adjudicate from a legal standpoint. While the oath, which was the best known part of Hippocrates' seminal work Hippocratic Corpus, has been modified or revised a number of times by different medical disciplines, the ethical implications of the oath are nevertheless always upheld, so much so that 1995 Nobel Peace Prize winner Joseph Rotblat suggested to have all scientists swear by it. Becoming a part of the profession, I recited the oath as I graduated from medical school and was accepted as a member of the medical community. It remains a rite of passage to majority in the medical profession as a guiding principle to a lifelong journey of learning and physical healing of the sick.

    To join the ranks of Aesculapius and Galen and Lister and even the well-known physicians of today always begins with the individual's view of oneself and what one wants to do with one's life and what it means for one's future. Medicine is an inspiring and a humanitarian profession. It is often that an individual wanting a career in medicine answers the question asked during a school interview that service to humanity propels him or her to seek the chance to be a doctor. It is a road paved with many diversions finally leading to a role with constant challenges in helping people, comforting them and allaying their fears, and giving hope even in the face of hopelessness and suffering. There is no other profession where the trust developed by human contact during the most vulnerable period of a patient's condition brings out the best of the physician's emotional fiber and character. Whether a doctor resolves to be a physician taking care of general health of a family or be a specialist undergoing further cognitive or interventional specialty of a chosen pathway, the profession demands intellectual stimulation and constantly keeping abreast of technical and scientific innovations for the benefit of the humanity it serves. Several years ago, I was asked to give a presentation by our local community college on Career Day to graduating high school seniors on what it takes to be a physician, being the only doctor on the Board of Regents. I mentioned all the difficulties of getting to become one and the advantages and the satisfaction of the experiences that follow afterward, though later I was not sure if any of those I give a talk to went for the lengthy process of becoming one. The appeal of other options where the course is much shorter and the financial rewards guarantee better security is one reason that leads me to this conclusion.

Not minimizing the importance and the humanism of other similar disciplines where further studies lead to being addressed as "Doctor," such as a chiropractor, optometrist, psychologist, or even a lawyer, a medical doctor does not think of the financial aspects brought about by the profession. Rather, it is the idea of a humanitarian endeavor that generates the will to walk the hallways of the hospital during the formative years, foregoing the tiredness and aching of an abused body and keeping all the five senses sharp at any given time. An internist professor of mine can tell while walking through a hallway and hearing a patient's cough that it was caused by a pneumococcal organism. At a well-known hospital where I did my surgical residency, the chief of surgery, a gentle transplant from South Africa, can diagnose almost to a certainty someone who has parathyroid disorder by looking at and examining the patient's fingernails. The clinical acumen developed during the past training and specialization was carried on to the touching, feeling, seeing, smelling, and hearing of patient's physical complaints. The rapid development of technical innovations, I think, has made newer medical students and residents, as well as doctors, have in their practice these advancements at the expense of the clinical faculties they possess and the inspiration and ideas they obtain from human interaction.

As much as it is a well-known tradition to have a physician-doctor relationship, modern times have highlighted and shown drawbacks not thought of or experienced by those seeking to be members of the profession. Consider that it is not fashionable or sacred nowadays to have this attachment, which has been abolished to an acceptable mnemonic of health-provider relationship. Doctors are no longer held in high regard or the same respect they had for many years. Patients demand that the newer sophisticated studies be used to diagnose and treat their illness even though in the best of a physician's judgment, the tests are not necessary. Newer doctors are beginning to realize that medicine is also a business that requires some degree of knowledge in running a practice, the like of which has never been mentioned or taught in medical school or in residency or fellowship programs. It is now being addressed by schools that offer executive MBA programs to physicians in an attempt to augment their business understanding in determining overhead, employee, and investment costs. To offset, though, the headaches of running a business, physicians are beginning to see the advantage of being an employee in the health care industry, or groups, individual practice organizations and accountable care organizations, retiring early rather than becoming and joining a dying breed of solo practitioners. The financial burden imposed by modest income and the temptations of being licensed to dispense prohibited substances not appropriately indicated for the disease process have resulted in some whose conviction smeared a noble profession. The accessibility of drugs prohibited from the general population but allowed to prescribing physicians has resulted as well in the doctors' substance abuse problems. While the reputation has suffered from the mistakes and unhappiness of a few, it does no justice for the high rate of suicide rates among any of the profession. It has been said that 300–400 physicians take their lives every year and that among the general population, the rate is similar between female and male doctors.

There was a time that doctors call the golden age of medicine, before the onset of current procedural codes and length-of-stay changes in the health care industry in the early '80s. Patients were confined and admitted to the hospital facility and discharged when they were deemed well, regardless of how long they stayed. Cost was not a factor then, until the health care cost was noted and projected to be a significant slice of federal budget if left "uncontrolled." It was the time that *City Hospital* was first televised as a medical drama in 1951, followed by *Dr. Kildare* and *Ben Casey* and the amiable Marcus Welby, whose bedside manner tackling both the common and uncommon cases as a family doctor was something to be emulated. *ER* was the longest TV series drama; *Grey's Anatomy* was resurrected a few years ago after its initial run of several seasons.

The continuous series of medical drama presently on TV screens, depicting human frailty and ministrations of a profession that remains necessary and relevant in this day and age reminds me that I chose the right course. I might not be in any cast, but I am still a doctor after all.

Charitable Organizations

I have a theory that I think is right more often than it is wrong. Every time I open my mail, it becomes bulkier, not because of the many important communications I am expecting, considering the bills I incur, but the ever-increasing charitable solicitations from many organizations I have not heard about. Of course, there are thousands and thousands of these charitable institutions all around the globe. But I notice that most of those I get have the same objectives. I suspect now that one organization that I gave my unconditional support initially shared my name and address to another, despite the protestations that come yearly of them not disclosing or sharing your identity. It has become my problem, and I suppose that of many as well, especially now because of my lingering suspicion, but the largest social media has admitted to selling my identity as well. Robocalls have added to the melee even if I subscribe and pay to have my name and my address removed or not included in any public directory. I do answer my calls if I am aware of who is at the other end of the line. And I give to charity without the responsible organization prodding me to write a contribution to a cause I believe in.

Charitable giving is a selfless act, unconditional in the compassion that comes with it and with the person extending it, not from the recognition it engenders but a conscious act of a selfless heart. It does not expect a reward in return. Thomas Aquinas, the common doctor of the Catholic Church, said, "Charity brings to life again those who are spiritually dead." Even in Islam, *sadaqah* is a term that is defined as an act of giving something to somebody without seeking a substitute in return. It has been shown by many research studies that we are much happier when we give than when we receive and that charitable giving puts a bigger smile on our face than what we spend on ourselves. It has a positive impact on our physical and mental health, contributing to a longer life. In a way while we aim to be selfless, we are also being selfish.

Which brings me to the point of what charitable organizations I will include in my list, what I am willing to give or donate to support the cause, and how much of the support I give actually goes to the intended recipients. Charity begins at home, as the saying goes, but we put aside some of the problems at home to attend to the more pressing issues that urgently demand our attention, such as hunger and disease in children, victims of wars and conflicts, natural disasters, and other catastrophes. These fundamental needs are sometimes seen in images on television and solicitation letters sent to potential donors. Of course, what we get and see are those that depict the dire situation the recipients are in and their need for kindness and love to help them.

There are a number of charitable organizations I include in my list. Although the number of charitable categories are innumerable, and this speaks of how humanity in general comes to the aid and assistance of those in need, I just have a number of causes that appeal to me and the limited pocketbook I balance at the end of the month, hoping that it is not overdrawn. I drop in the two envelopes every weekend I attend church services and sometimes the campaigns the church undertakes every so often. It is not necessarily the 10 percent tithe of the income or profits earned everyone expects but rather the amount my budget can afford. While I am aware that the church I belong to is believed to be engulfed in wealth no one could possibly imagine, it does not prevent me from subsidizing the many religious and the worldwide evangelization and propagation of my faith by the good works it does. My wife also does charitable activities related to some activities of the church, spending some time when she is needed. Having a background in the medical field and knowing that the government could not itself wrap around the many facets of research designed to find the cure of certain diseases, a donation to a health organization such as the American Kidney Foundation, the Diabetes Action Research Foundation, the American Lung Association, or the American Cancer Society have become recipients of medical donations for the continuous efforts for public benefit. Looking at the faces of children in sub-Saharan desert and in many famine-ravaged countries in the world brings me to respond to this calamity with a check in an envelope signed, sealed, and delivered to the organization demanding my help. My late father, who was in the army during World War II, and my father-in-law, who until his death at 103 1/2 four years ago, had some family members in the military, including my stint during the Vietnam War, make me partial to the women and men who fought and died the longest battle we have raging now. Many war veteran categories have been set up to help those lucky to return despite the physical disabilities incurred during their deployment. It is no wonder that despite the solicitation envelopes scattered over my oversized desk, I always reach out first for those that have to do with helping disabled veterans. And it is not only to one but several that I give what little I can. In kind, a group of similar-minded folks and I travel once a year to Third World countries, donating our time, talent, and treasure mending the broken health of patients who can't afford the services of health professionals and the bureaucracy of a government that says it cares but cannot give any material assistance to alleviate the ill health of its indigent citizens. Charitable giving takes on many forms, not only the money donated for what cause an individual determines deserves his or her most help. Giving up one's seat to an older person left standing on a bus rail, carrying the shopping bag of someone who finds the load heavier than she or he could carry, treating people working for you with respect and consideration is more charity than can be stuffed in an envelope with postage attached to it.

It is said that among the countries in the world, the United States leads in giving to charitable causes, responding to calamities worldwide. The assistance it provides and the relief it brings are self-imposed, being the richest and most dominant power to extend its hand where it is needed. I still check, though, on whether the small pocket change I give to the causes I believe in is going to the intended recipients. Thus, I always check the charitable organizations and how much of the fundraising goes to charities, the professional fundraisers it employs, the operating costs, and the compensation of those who are chosen to lead the campaign. I might not be Bill Gates or Warren Buffett or measure up to Oprah Winfrey and the worldwide charitable organizations their foundations support to reduce the sufferings of this world. But the philanthropy they all espouse is on a larger scale. Mine is just a drop in the ocean.

Weather

There is an ongoing debate involving all the countries in the world. And despite the many conferences, agreements, and pacts surrounding the conflicting points by the international community regarding climate change and its effects on the earth and human existence, it remains a volatile subject and still unsettled. The two sides of the argument believe their arguments prevail. The preoccupation with the climate changes such as global warming, loss of sea ice, rise of sea levels, more droughts and stronger storms, and all the implications for planet Earth's cycle and survival began in the early nineteenth century when carbon dioxide and methane gases were first suspected and the so-called greenhouse gases were noted to change the earth's climate. Both were noted to increase Earth's surface temperature. It was later found to increase by approximately 1.8 °F since that time, the change in atmospheric levels agreed by both sides. And because the CO_2 and methane gases absorb some of the heat released by the sun and is then bounced back to Earth, it warms up the planet, causing a greenhouse effect.

If you are on the side that subscribes to the variously explained scientific findings and opinion of the warming causing recent severe havoc experienced globally, then greenhouse emissions need to be reduced by curtailing human activities such as burning fossil fuels, aerosols, architectural improvizations, and any that cause a human-generated atmospheric warming. Climate change and especially global warming and its oceanic processes, despite the tectonic shift from an earthquake in the Indian Ocean, have been blamed as the cause of the deadly tsunami in 2004 in Thailand that resulted in more than 4,812 dead and 8,457 injured. More than 4,000 people are still unaccounted for from this disaster. The frequent tsunami in Japan, the volcanic eruptions in several parts of the globe, the storms and droughts in several areas of the world and the Midwest floods that result from arguably these climate changes convince the scientists and meteorologists' influential studies and experimental measurements about the fluctuations and the changes brought about by human activities. People like the physicist John Tyndall who discovered that CO_2 absorbs sun's heat. Guy Callender demonstrated that fossil combustion and the increase in atmospheric CO_2 cause global warming. Charles Keating in 1958 while working at an observatory in Hawaii, made measurements that confirmed the levels of atmospheric CO_2 were increasing. James Hansen of NASA testified before the US Senate about the direct effect of CO_2 on the planet.

Some have argued that human-generated greenhouse gas emissions are so small, and the earth or the planet can absorb the increases. After all, the world has been in existence for a billion years and has been subjected to fluctuations in the natural processes as radiation, eruptions, ocean currents, alterations induced by discernible forces. To many, the human-caused global catastrophes that we are witnessing now are based on "questionable measurements, faulty climate models and misleading science." Richard Lindzen, an MIT meteorologist, argued that the findings by the scientific community, the computerized models were deemed unreliable and any CO_2, projected to increase by 25 percent by the end of the century by John Sawyer, would ultimately balance out. A report that came out charging that climate change is "a global public health problem" earned a rebuke from US Senator James Inhofe (R-OK) who stated, "We can all agree that natural variations in the climate are taking place, but man-made global warming still remains a theory."

Among Americans, 73 percent think that global warming is happening, while 14 percent do not believe that it is. Along party lines, 95 percent of Democrats think global warming is a problem that the country has to face, with it being caused by 84 percent of the human population. On the other hand, only 40 percent of Republicans believe that it is part of the ideological spectrum and only 26% attributes it to human activities. This much can be said however: whatever extreme political persuasion people in the United States belong to, both agree that human activities and warming are occurring.

In June 2017, President Trump withdrew the United States from the Paris Agreement signed by 195 countries in December 2015. The agreement's aim was to prevent global temperatures from rising more than 1.5 degrees to 2 degrees Celsius above pre-industrial levels. Finding that there were a few countries who were signatory to the pact who were exempted or not following the provisions of the agreement, the president, citing these and other economic burdens to energy development to this country, pulled out from the agreement. While the United States is the only known signatory who has withdrawn from the pact, its practical implications remain to be seen.

There are several predictions advanced by knowledgeable people, some whose viewpoints regarding statistical weather patterns and its distributions continue to stimulate the debate about the climate change. Whether catastrophic weather events such as the depth of the ocean, the direction of the currents, rainfall or drought and scarcity of rain in some parts of the world, the breaking of centuries-old icebergs and ice floes, vegetation involving plants and animals, are still unknown impacts of an evolving science of climate change.

I did not mean to get involved and put myself in an ongoing debate on climate change. I only intended to mention how the weathermen or weatherwomen I see every night when I listen to the newscast predict what the weather would look like the rest of the day or the rest of the week. I am fascinated by the graphics and the weather patterns over much of the country in an eight-minute weather segment, and how they do it. To that, I think of the many weather satellites we have now in the sky circling and the historical connotation knowing what the weather is like before a big battle, unlike the Battle of Trebbia River:

not knowing then what the weather was, Hannibal sent his soldiers to a freezing river for no good reason. I resent the condescension, however, when the meteorologist, after saying that the temperature outside is five degrees below zero, tells me to bundle up to keep myself warm whenever I go out. I need not be reminded of what to wear or do. Otherwise, I would just heed the advice of an old raconteur who says that if you want to find out whether it is raining outside, do get out and feel the raindrops.

I would rather carry an umbrella though rain or shine, just like my wife does.

The Fourth Estate

I have always been under the impression that the fourth estate referred to the press and the news media, which includes those news gumshoes with pencils wedged between their ears and their heads, radio or television people with their thrust microphones who struggle with a mob to get a comment or even capture sound bites from the newsmaker of the day for the six o'clock news. While these news hounds do not represent a part of a political system, the institution they belong to holds a significant influence in framing the issues of the day and the capacity to stay on and influence what the direction of the government should be, which sometimes turns out to be the opposite of what they want it to be.

I did not consider myself as a member of this gentrified tradition when I was appointed as editor in chief of *Nursery Whispers*, a high school newsmagazine still steeped in the old stencil for reproducing the articles submitted for publication. Mrs. Macaraeg, my high school teacher in social studies did not think so as well, as we were just a small school paper with local coverage within the boundaries of our school. It was a little different when the dean of the university college of liberal arts chose me as a section editor of a quarterly magazine and finally I was selected after a competitive exam as a roving reporter of the monthly campus newspaper that occasionally strayed off into local politics, wielding influence in the form of student talk and discussion at coffee shops on and off campus. It was then I started believing that after all I was a card-carrying member of the fourth estate, even though it identified me as just a campus journalist and not a national newspaper reporter.

I seldom hear the term nowadays. As a matter of fact, I have not heard it mentioned in recent years, this term attributed to an Edmund Burke, an English parliamentarian at a debate in 1787 in the House of Commons. While earlier reports of it being a derivation of the traditional concept of clergy, nobility, and commoners, the term has been variously applied to a number of groups and lay people including lawyers, clergy, and political activists. As to when the term finally was distilled and accepted to mean what is now known as the press, the year was probably more than a century ago when the term *journalist* was applied to William Cobbett in 1821 by William Hazlitt, whose son was an editor of a Frenchman who advocated bribery to buy favorable verdicts for the wealthy at the expense of rightful litigants.

In the United States, lately has the country been polarized by competing viewpoints, and the press replaced by technological innovation called social media. Oscar Wilde wrote many years ago about the press and journalism, which was then dominating the events of the day. The press and journalism that he was talking about in the old days now have been replaced by social media, which, by all indications, have not emphasized the independence it is supposed to project. This conclusion, however, depends on whatever side of the discourse one is on, although the present atmosphere remains, as is the perception of almost everyone, that the country is divided.

Social media are web-based sites that allow people to interact almost instantaneously with one another. It is a forum where people of similar or dissimilar interests can comment or discuss any idea or topic, give an opinion on anything. It can elevate a discourse or sink a person, depending on how the conversation is considered positive or negative. And it is worldwide. Human minds and the evolution of progress and civilization bring to reality what was once unthinkable. But every progress forward carries a regressive step backward. Nowhere is this brought to the forefront than that experienced by Facebook, a social media that has 2.3 billion users worldwide. Its founder, Mark Zuckerberg, has been asked to testify before the US Congress and explain why there appears to be a slant toward one side of the equation at the expense of another. In Europe, the social giant's problems are piling up, with possible sanctions and regulations, as it was found that it had the data of its subscribers available to third parties without the apparent consent of its customers. The other social media sites that have replaced with speed the slow crawl of the old fourth estate and are facing regulatory actions that are coming fast from abroad include web sites such as YouTube, WhatsApp, Instagram, Google, and Twitter, to name a few. The problems of these modalities of bringing the news instantaneously as it occurs has led to the introduction of a social code of practice for broadcasters, telecommunications, and mainstream as well as cable media. Implementing these series of mandatory terms of service and requirements, however, is not at all presently assured. One can only turn to the pages of a printed media or turn on what the anchors and analysts' analysis of the day's events and see what entrenchment to an opinion everyone still has.

There are still many issues that social media, as it is called, faces, such as embedding in political advocacy organizations. It has replaced what I have known as the basic function of the fourth estate, later known as the press, in digging out the truth, no matter if it were a tedious and slow process before presenting it to its readership, who renders its own judgment. Truth is a relative term to most people. But whether it is absolute or relative, facts are understood pieces of information that make an assertion believed to be true.

There is no turning back. But progress for its own sake sometimes carries with it changes that do not justify the means to an end.

Marriage

I have just been to a relative's wedding. It was that of the granddaughter of my late brother and his wife, both of whom have passed away, seventeen and eighteen years ago respectively. I have only seen his granddaughter twice in my lifetime, once when she was five years old and the other when she was a teenager, before she left her parents ostensibly for a man whom she met at a dancing school. I have never met her groom, and if you were to ask me if I would recognize both of them casually at any encounter, I would not know who they were. It was for my late brother Jim that I accepted his eldest daughter's invitation. The wedding ceremony was stupendous, and the reception was grand for the bride and the groom, both of whom now reside in Switzerland, although the marriage was arranged and performed in New Jersey. I never met or was introduced to the newlyweds, only the mother; the eldest daughter of my late brother approached me and my wife, and I suppose the rest of the remaining twelve of us brothers and sisters at the wedding. It probably was not the bride and the groom's fault that we have not been as close to them as we are to the rest of our relatives. It was probably because we did not seek her or her groom out when we should have. Anyhow, I am going to another nephew's wedding in one week. The son of my sister is a close nephew, having slept at their house many times over and encouraging him to become a doctor when he joined our surgical mission during his undergraduate days in college. Two different circumstances for similar occasions for two relatives.

The marriage I attended, however, made me appreciate this old-fashioned contract of a man and a woman who commit themselves to be husband and wife and desire for the union to last a lifetime. It is a very important decision to take with the hope that a long-lasting relationship produces a lovely family, has children, and a promise to care for each other for the rest of the whole life. This institution, which was initially codified in the eleventh century mostly in central Europe but practiced in the cultural valleys of Mesopotamia in earlier times, were not because man and a woman were in love but arranged by families for economic reasons, granting of property rights, and protection of bloodlines. The Catholic Church confirmed it as a sacrament in the Council of Trent on March 1547, reaffirming what was believed to be a religious union between a man and a woman in 1184. Although the figures in 2018 still show that 50 percent of marriages in the United States end in a divorce or separation, it is encouraging that this rate is dropping because of the millennials' changing attitudes toward marriage. Marriage is highest in Massachusetts, while Oklahoma leads in divorce rates. Internationally, Luxembourg with its population pegged at half a million has the highest divorce rate in the world (87% percent), followed surprisingly by Spain (65 percent), a predominantly Catholic country, While it is often the belief that sexual infidelity after a while in the relationship is the cause of the breakup, surprisingly the leading reason from a recent poll for the split has been communication problems. Among the professions where the divorce rate is noted to be high are massage therapists, gaming workers, flight attendants, vocational nurses.

The concept of marriage only as a heterosexual institution was challenged on constitutional grounds later on and has roiled every state in the union since the Supreme Court of Hawaii in 1993 ruled in favor of a same-sex couple whose rights were supposedly violated under the law, where there was no clear definition of the partnership. Fearing that the ruling might be a threat detrimental to the society, the US Congress in 1996 passed the Defense of Marriage Act (DOMA) confirming the traditional definition of marriage as between a woman and a man and demanding that for purposes of federal recognition and issuance of benefits, states in the union are not allowed to recognize same-sex marriage performed in other states. Those that supported the original idea as was intended invoked religious doctrines and biblical exegesis, but eventually as public debate continued and many states found support regarding same-sex marriages, DOMA was finally declared unconstitutional. In several attempts to justify the same-sex union, it was variously labeled as civil union, domestic partnership, or marital arrangement. Historically marriage between same sexes was recorded between the Roman emperor Nero and another man, as was in 1061 in a small chapel in Spain. Finally, on January 2015, the US Supreme Court in *Oberfell v. Hodges* legalized same-sex marriage in all fifty states.

While marriages are interpreted and performed in different cultures, an old-fashioned guy like me still adheres to a one-man, one-woman genre, witnessed by a few, performed by someone ordained or legally recognized to conduct the ceremony—something like the one I had many years ago, though as not as grand as the recent one I attended. Some marriages I know barely lasted longer than the wedding ceremony. While this conclusion could be an exaggeration at times, I know of some where the parents of the bride spent lavishly for the wedding, only to witness later the disintegration of a onetime love affair, an irretrievable and irreconcilable breakdown that only the couple involved knew anything about, and more often than not, they would not divulge openly the reasons for the split. It is a fact that every thirteen seconds in the United States, a divorce is happening, equating to 277 per hour. In a recent study, it was found that the lowest divorce rate was among Asians, followed by Hispanics.

There are many types of marriages these days other than the traditional marriage. There is same-sex marriage, interracial marriage, common-law marriage, monogamous or polygamous marriage such as it exists in other cultures, civil, and a host of many other permutations. In one recent trip to China, I was surprised by the number of wives called concubines a Chinese emperor could have. Women then were forever kept in seclusion only to be summoned at the behest of the emperor. This does not happen now that societal mores and systems have changed. In some areas of the world, women were allowed as well to have multiple husbands at a given time.

In the early '70s, one of my senior surgical residents was a Japanese man who happened at that time to be single. Every year, he went back to Japan to choose among the women his parents had selected would be a good wife for him. He always came back not committed to any of his parents' choices. I never found out whether he finally succumbed to this Japanese custom of arranged marriages, which were practiced by less than 5 percent then. But I was privy to the wedding of a couple of Indian descent in early 2012 when I was still practicing in the panhandle of Texas. The couple did not meet or see each other until the day of their wedding, which was arranged by their respective parents, who were then residing in Alabama. Obviously, it was not a forced marriage as distinguished from an arranged marriage, as both consented and presumably had the assistance of their parents in making the match. The union produced a wonderful daughter, a thriving restaurant and hotel business, a developed love and liking for one another, and most of all, the family became our patients.

If the wedding that I am going to next week in Virginia, of my nephew who is marrying an Iranian obstetrician-gynecologist, ends up like my former Indian couple so far, although the marriage is not arranged, I would not bat an eyelash, no matter that the marriage ceremony is different from what I had half a century back.

05/07/2019

History Revisited

Hanging on a wall in my office is a 4″ × 12″ wooden frame that is inscribed in longhand an aphorism that I always take heed every day. It reads, "Don't forget where you came from but never lose the sight of where you are going." I saw this frame with the inscription over a blue sky and under it a railroad track at one of the stores as I wandered over to the heap in the single-items section while waiting for my wife to make her usual selection of what I consider a not-too-necessary purchase. It has become a part of the collection of paraphernalia I have had since I was still in grade school. It includes all the books written and writings of the national hero of the country I came from, the articles and pictures I came across reading about the history of world civilization and the progress coming to this century, and everything I could lay my eyes and hands on the subject I developed an interest on. It also has an amalgamation of trivia related to the historical birth of the independent nation I migrated to almost a half a century ago. The parchment of the Declaration of Independence, the Bill of Rights, the traditional and fearless leaders of the American Revolution, the Civil War between the states, and the march to the present are all included in both the historical recollection and tangible materials I possess. Ask me about the First or Second Amendments, or the Twenty-fifth Amendment mentioned almost daily by pundits these days and I can quote verbatim what these amendments are. What is constitutional or not, I easily refer to the copy I have if I am not certain what the reference is all about.

But reading and looking at countless pictures of where this country came from the present and the future where it might be destined to go, is not as real as when you walk through the grounds where some of the history was made. Two weeks ago, attending the wedding ceremony of a nephew in Virginia we made a beeline on two successive cloudy and rainy days to the Heritage Plantation of the fifth president of the republic, James Monroe, and Monticello, the little mountain retreat and plantation of his mentor and an author of the Declaration of Independence, Thomas Jefferson, the third president of the United States, which originally consisted of the thirteen continental states. Both were called plantations, consisting of hundreds of acres or rolling hills and valleys, their stately homes, and the buildings, some of which have been restored to what these looked like during the centuries preceding their tenures as leaders of the independence movement. How daring and brave these men in their resolve about the inequities of colonial British empire despite the feral determination of their colonial masters to subjugate their New World subjects, was not lost on the guides, who provided a running prologue and epilogue to the tourists who signed up on a wet and drizzly day to hear the perspectives in those days. What I did not know was what the thirteen presidents mentioned in the book by Kenneth C. Davis, owned enslaved people in their households when all were fighting for independence, liberty, basic rights, and the rule of law from the "lobsters" or "bloodybacks" as the Redcoats or British soldiers were called by the colonists. Only John Adams, the second president, and his son John Quincy Adams, the sixth president, thought that slavery was wrong and did not own any slaves. Woodrow Wilson, who was the twenty-eighth president in 1913, was the last to hold enslaved people; many presidents did not release or grant freedom to the slaves they owned, even at their deathbeds. It has been said that Jefferson had more than six hundred slaves and enslaved people, though he released less than four or five before he died penniless and almost a pauper. Only in recent memory was his manly humanity revealed in his secret dalliance with his favored slave Sally Hemmings, who was in her teens when she had a child with Thomas Jefferson. Although I knew beforehand how slaves were trapped and caught in Africa, brought in galleys across the oceans, and auctioned off in different markets in the New World, where each one became property of the owner. I was not aware of how it was to be a slave for the rest of your life. But now I know the deeper meaning of Martin Luther's march in Selma and his quintessential speech in Washington DC and the drive toward civil rights and the recent call of additional reparative measures. If the past is remembered and the present and the future are to be the motivations of a country thought to be the greatest in the history of mankind, the additional call for reparations personally, to my thinking, is not to be made a priority anymore.

There is some trivia I learned from these two days in the hills of Virginia and the visit to the epochal retreats of the two presidents of the republic. The beds were four-postered and canopied and feathered. The rooms, though the mansions were considered stately, were small, and there were no comfort rooms adjacent or attached. Thomas Jefferson and James Monroe as well as the retinue in their family and their guests, relieved themselves in an outhouse or in a commode provided in their rooms. While both were tall, the size of the beds though it was mentioned by the guides that they were as large as the king size in today's measurements, appeared small. People in those days slept almost in a sitting position with their heads up, as it was a customary belief that lying flat was for people who were dead, a tradition that European monarchy fostered and carried across to the New World.

Security detail as it exists today, consisting of dark eye-glassed Secret Service agents, was not provided to very important people in those days. Monroe and Jefferson had to fend for themselves in their travels and movements across the country and abroad. It was not mentioned, nevertheless, whether they were subjected to attempts on their well-being.

I have been to Andrew Jackson's Hermitage Plantation in Tennessee and hopefully in my next travels, I would visit Mount Vernon and Montpellier. If there is anything to be learned from revisiting history, it is that one can't always grasp the importance of a historical event or its impact on recalling what it was and the relevance it has on the future.

Mentorship

Several weeks ago, I received a letter from the Department of Veterans Affairs. In it was a survey asking me if I was currently involved in any teaching or mentorship roles and, if so, in what capacity. I paused for a moment before I thought of writing back. If teaching means what I used to do before I retired—making rounds with interns and residents, telling them what I would have learned and experienced so far in my capacity as someone higher up on a totem pole as an attending or a professor in a hospital and medical school, I would have answered as George H. W. Bush used to say, "been there, done that." If it involves giving lectures and talks of conditions related to medicine and the subject matter of which I haven't yielded any cognitive abilities, I would have answered that I was still teaching. The fact of the matter is, despite what everyone calls retirement after many years of active clinical practice, I still continue to attend surgical meetings, brush up on what is new and different in my field of surgery, and even give talks and lectures to professional groups who might find out that I still know what I am talking about. Involvement at one time or another in the Traveling Fellow Program of our surgical society, showing and teaching a fully trained surgeon from the Philippines what are supposed to be new techniques of how things are done in the US, I consider a part of teaching, albeit to someone already steeped in the medical and surgical field.

But mentorship, to my mind, is different. It is giving experienced advice, the pros and cons to someone who has yet to decide what in life one would become or pursue. It dawned on me that despite the haze of statistics we accumulate, the myriad of patients that we see in underserved areas where we are invited to go on the yearly surgical missions we undertake, and the unfamiliarity of these places and the hospitals we do our operations, we seem to neglect the impact our surgical society and the event have on those students and the nonmedical personnel who come along with us. While most of the students that tag along with these missions have not firmly committed to going the way doctors and surgeons have, coming out and back from the experience, they gain from the humanity of it all, they see and solidify their resolve to enter one day the medical field and the profession.

Sometimes, while some have already chosen the life and the profession they intend to follow, they join the missions to explore and find out about a foreign place and foreign people, and come back with a newfound belief that doctors who undertake these missions are human after all and not tied to the worrisome problems encountered at home in the USA. While the perception exists that relationships between lawyers and physicians are mostly adversarial in nature, it did not manifest itself during the time that the surgical society was in Legaspi many years ago. It is well to know that somehow an activity such as this promotes the idea that there are still those who believe that charity to the less fortunate is a much higher calling.

Several years ago, the Society of Philippine Surgeons in America had five, among the many volunteers, join the surgical mission: two students and a newly married couple, newly minted lawyers temporarily working in Palau. One student, a first-generation Chinese-American who has been with the society on several missions, and the two lawyers joined the mission to Legaspi, which the year before was devastated by havoc following the eruption of the perfectly coned volcano in the city. Eric Mallack and his classmate in undergraduate school in Pennsylvania joined the group as well. I later asked Eric, one of the lawyers, and Tina, the first-generation Chinese-American to write about their experiences after the mission and what they thought of the endeavor, their interaction with some of the doctors who mentored them, encouraged and explained to them what the undertaking was all about. The essays the three wrote were published in an earlier issue of the *Philippine Surgeon* magazine.

Many years later, in going through the older issues of the magazine, I thought that the essays were timely even up to now, as the society continues to mount these mission forays in places for the second, third, or fourth time. I found out that a reprint was as refreshing as it was the first time these observations by the three volunteers were written. The essays were reprinted in another issue of the magazine. Eric graduated from Temple University School of Medicine and had another degree in a related field at the University of Pennsylvania. He finished his pediatric residency and a fellowship in pediatric neurology at Presbyterian and Cornell, where he joined the faculty and works as an attending in the hospital. His classmate Craig went to UDMJ Johnson School of Medicine and is now a physiatrist establishing his own center and clinic. Tina went to medical school in Washington DC, did an OB-GYN residency in New York and Nashville. She is now in practice in Elk Grove, Illinois. As for Ben Carter, the lawyer who masterfully kept all the mission doctors on their schedule, he returned to Louisville, Kentucky, and formed his own law firm that specializes in consumer law and teaches at a university law school. He and his former wife Erin, presently a federal prosecutor, went their separate ways though they both remain on good terms. He is now married to Sarah, a nurse practitioner with whom he has two children.

There are many more of these stories of nonmedical personnel, of undergraduate students who come and join our yearly surgical missions eventually finding their calling. It is teaching but more of mentoring in which I still am involved. The medical field is not filled up or overpopulated, no matter what others might think. It could use some more people and mentors who find that rendering service in a sanitized and perfect environment is not at all uncommon.

> *Great leaders don't tell you what to do . . . they show you how it is done.*
>
> *(Reprinted from the Philippine Surgeon, Letter from the Editor column)*

Change and Leadership

It has been called the spice of life. Each day is different from the previous day. Sometimes the change is subtle and imperceptible to others; at times, it presents itself as obviously as the sun rising from the east. Changes that take place in nature are things we can't control. We can't switch the time the tide comes or the direction of the wind when it blows though we can change the direction of the sails as they say.

But there are changes where we can exercise some degree of control, where others can guide and show us possible outcomes. Witness the shuffle or reshuffle in the political and social fabric that includes our own personal life. While changes in the government from time to time do not come as a surprise to everyone and are often viewed with some degree of suspicion, in the life of an organizational structure such as those that are abundant in our society, both for-profit and nonprofit, these changes come as an assertion for the better. They are made to prolong the existence of an organization or corporation that wants to stay relevant in the present and the future when some are folding because of financial woes, membership attrition, and inability to adapt and change their mission. It is widely acknowledged that the success of an organization in large measure depends on who its leader is. Successful organizations have at the helm someone who, according to Jack Welch, the former CEO and chairman of General Electric, "creates a vision, articulates the vision, passionately owns the vision, and relentlessly drives it to completion." It is important not only to provide the input but also to come out with a positive output. Organizations grow and flourish when they are guided by effective leaders. The bystander effect that sometimes exists within a group or organization tends to diminish with a leader who shares the power of his office *with* not *over* the members, in a reciprocal relationship. A leader should not have or focus on his or her personal agenda at the expense of the organization that he or she leads, as is prevalent in some that are exposed doing this today.

It is true that we cannot isolate ourselves from what is changing and happening around us. The direction we and organizations need to take depends on what confronts us, whether it be on a local, national, or worldwide order. It depends on the circumstances, present or, more importantly, what is predicted for the future. What policies enunciated and undertaken by a country or government in power that deals with matters like tax reform, tax-exempt status to nonprofit entities, adoption and promulgation of laws that affects the citizens, and yes, even restrictions imposed on what constitutes the country's borders and immigration policies, affect organizations, corporations and societies that deal with problems like these.

Nowhere is it as abundantly clear that a different approach has to be changed or tried by the government, organizations, or bureaucracies on an issue such as health care demanding a different solution now that it has become a socioeconomic problem of a burgeoning population. Consider that even though the US spends approximately 16 percent of its GDP, second highest to East Timor among the United Nations member nations and spends twice as much on health care per capita than any other country, it ranks forty-third in mortality rate, with approximately 30,000 infants dying each year, the mortality related to the health of the mother, other public health practices, socioeconomic conditions, and the availability of appropriate health care for infants and pregnant women. Health care costs have grown so much faster than wages or inflation in the past decade, causing budget deficits of several trillion dollars projected within the next few years. Many have variously stated that the number of people that do not have health insurance in this country is between

30 and 47 million of the more than 300 million population. It was supposed to be remedied by the changes in the Affordable Care Act, though it appears the problems were not totally solved. It is presently an argument addressed by the present administration.

While there is much to argue about the necessity of health care reform in the country and the many ways parties are offering different solutions, the delivery of health care worldwide and to those underserved areas are carried out by many altruistic and charitable groups, foundations, and organizations, these despite some resistance from the government bureaucracies and organized groups in the countries where the missions are involved. The financial constraints faced by these organizations, especially those that are not established and funded by foundations of the well-to-do, have to dig a little bit deeper into their individual coffers for the additional costs normally borne by mission sponsors and hosts who are experiencing shortfall of funds. The efforts periodically and continually undertaken are subject to changes in local, national, and international levels faced by those that get involved in humanitarian endeavors. If the changes needed are not appropriately met in a constantly changing environment and the organization remains static in its approach to the problems it faces, then it would eventually fail and fold. This outcome is not predicated on an assumption but on real experiences.

Any attempts by any organization to singlehandedly minimize or prevent 17 million people worldwide dying yearly from infectious, surgical diseases and from natural calamities is not practical and not really achievable. But its leadership can continue to make a dent in these tragic phenomena and educate the public about the necessity of changes in any problem it faces.

Identity

Securing anonymity especially from unwanted intruders to your privacy have been a preoccupation I have always strived for and coveted. As a consequence, I have always subscribed to, albeit as an additional option, not have my name and address published in the residential pages of the local telephone directory. I have also asked that the landline phones I have at home not be accessible except to some people I am familiar with. And the smartphone directive that isolates those that do not want to be subjects of promotional calls or robocalls is scrupulously followed by me to the core. But I found out that no matter what the options you signed up and paid for or following and removing your name from the smartphone list for unwanted calls is only a short-lived performance. I suppose it is partly my own fault, filling up the forms for any registration I signed that requires listing my phone, both landline and cell phones, address, or my e-mail lest it would be deemed incomplete. But these establishments not in the business of disclosure share your identity and pertinent information to their cohorts, generally of the same business as they are, no matter that they send you their yearly privacy disclosures mentioning that they do not share what information they gathered about their customers or clients with anyone. But I still maintain that it is not completely my fault that some people and business and promotional groups and mostly unidentifiable establishments get to dial or send me unwanted notifications or messages I do not have use for or care about. I refuse to get up and answer an unfamiliar and unidentified caller or mail that dials me up or write even to this day, despite knowing what I know now. If there are others to be blamed, it is the companies where I signed up for the nondisclosure options at the beginning of the contract.

With the new technology and its continuous advances in what is illegal as an antidote to what is allowed, it becomes useless to try and remain anonymous these days. Though I cling to the concept that I personally could remain anonymous to people and groups whose attention I want to be immune from, I still remain signed up for the options I still subscribed to. The dark web, as it has been called, located in some known and unknown places in the world, penetrates the identity of anyone that it wants. Mention the firewalls that surround the Office of the US President, the National Security Council and the way it conducts its communications, sensitive governmental bureaucracies, and many more organizations, and one finds out that secrets no longer remain inviolate but can be exposed at will. I was, as everyone else, I assume, surprised at the recent acknowledgment by the Securities and Exchange Commission that the general public is sick and tired of being bombarded by unwanted robocalls. I was under the impression that this government agency had promulgated a long time ago to have companies block these calls to subscribers of the service. The ruling it recently issued in May 2019 in this war on calls that violate the identity of subscribers blocks calls by default before they reach the home phones or mobile devices of 152.9 million people each day, provisions that I continue to sign up for as a consumer. Of course, companies that take advantage of these new technologies known as spam called for reconsideration of the increased FCC attention to the plight of the consumers. Blocking fraudulent call identification is still not free, and caller ID remains a convenient option to those that can afford it and the few who are lucky enough not to attract the attention of scam artists and the dark web that they inhabit.

Identity and the activity appended to it has become an industry that prevents it from happening. Thus, identity-theft companies have spawned a new conglomeration of industries that purportedly protect anyone that is concerned about the preservation of personal data such as phone numbers, date of birth, address, e-mail, and the more important Social Security Administration number. It requires, however, divulging these data to the identity-theft provider, which assiduously claims to protect these from falling into the prying eyes of someone, guaranteeing legal protection with an inordinate sum of money should the breach happens. It makes one to think twice, like myself, to avail of this identity protection to disclose pertinent information to an entity whose aim is to keep them secret. Once I attempted to enroll in one of the identity-theft companies, but the idea of providing the required set of information about me to secure anonymity turned me off. Risky as it is, I would take my chances with the establishments I originally and continuously to this day trust to hide my identity despite the breaches of confidentiality I experience almost every day. And I will hold the FCC to its recent promise to the American people that it hears their concerns and the message that the new ruling is on the consumers' side.

There is another form of identity lately that differs from the data of an individual protected from unwanted exposure that is expressed by visual and print media. Conjugated to identity is the term *politics*, which results in a strong appeal especially to millennials, who occupy the forefront of discussion and influence in a rapidly changing culture. It is called *identity politics*, which the dictionary defines as "politics in which groups of people having a particular racial, religious, ethnic, social or cultural identities tend to promote their own specific interests or concerns without regard to the interest or concerns of any larger political group." It is a group with historical assertion that looks under the prism of past and present social injustice and the grievances committed to a meaningful group whose mission is to "explore and act out." Balancing and compromising on issues that affect society is anathema to these groups that suddenly feel the effects of belonging to different class of gender, race, religion, and class. The movement remains a potent force nowadays that any form of identity, whether individual or groupthink, should include identitarian goals and agenda.

While the rhetoric it brings to the context of political life remains combustible, no matter which side you are on, whether you are for or against what is presently dividing our country, I pine for the type of identity that makes my personal life remain anonymous.

Pursuit of Anything

Fishing

I am not much of a fisherman. At least, I do not consider myself a part of humanity who belongs to one of the oldest occupations of mankind. But I know that when I go fishing, I know what I am fishing for, unlike Henry David Thoreau, who one day said, "Many men go fishing all their lives without knowing that it is not fish they are after." I know that fishing makes your life much longer especially if you fire up the pan and cook what you catch from fresh or salt water. After all, was it Paul Dudley White, that eminent cardiologist to President Eisenhower, who extolled the virtues of eating what swims and flies to ones that walk on all fours? I think this is still a truism in this day and age.

    I got hooked on fishing one day when my wife and I, in the early '70s, drove from New York to neighboring Connecticut to spend the weekend with a couple who were then and now considered friends. In a spur of a moment when we ran out of something to do, Arthur pulled his hook, line, and sinker and coaxed me to tackle the stream where he generally spent his spare time when he was not dissecting dead people at the morgue. You see, he was a pathology resident, and this was part of his job, aside from finding what medical adventures could have been done to prevent a corpus from the cold freezer. His wife, who was training to be an anesthesiologist, and their two daughters—one of whom we were lucky enough to call our goddaughter—most of the time spared him his fatherly duties.

He mentioned perch as a freshwater fish he generally caught. Sometimes he took home one or two blue pikes, the result of his casting his lines till it was dark. We never used any device such as gill nets or seines, thus we never caught any pelagic haul and went home with the tale and a lame excuse that we nevertheless had fun. No fish meal that night except what we consumed in a nearby restaurant.

The bug caught me so much so that several weeks later on a weekend, I drove to Sheepshead Bay in Brooklyn not too far away, where we had an apartment. After watching a few hardened fish hunters (I was able to tell by their mien) and some neophytes who were dragged into that charter fishing boat by well-meaning friends whom I assumed were there for the adventure, I finally gathered my nerves to board and sail to claim my share of what the boat captain promised to everyone, an abundance of anadromous catch, of striped bass and stripers, a few miles into the Atlantic Ocean. I have never gone to what everybody calls deep-sea fishing, but on that day, I was proud of the experience I appropriated for myself. I even promised my wife that I would bring back home the harvest from the sea.

Five miles into the ocean when the captain told everyone to throw in their hand lines, their hooks and sinkers, the waters became so choppy. The boat waved and listed that I became nauseous, and short of projectile vomiting what I had for breakfast that morning, I just ran to the small cabin and never cast the pole I was provided. I do not know what the others did for the three hours we were out, but I could not care less. I returned home wobbly from the trip. What was even more pathetic was me coming home empty-handed, unable to fulfill my promise.

I thought that it would be much calmer to fish if one has to divert from the salt water of an ocean to the reaches of streams or rivers. After all, inland fishing is contained abundantly in such rivers as Mississippi or St. Lawrence in North America, at the Danube, Dnieper, or Volga in Europe. Several anglers and occasional fishermen like me started watching every week. Jimmy Houston, hauling and patting on the head then releasing the bass he caught, became an avid convert to the sport. The only difference between him and me is that whatever I caught inevitably ends up a meal and not back in the water.

So it is not any wonder that when we settled in the great republic of Texas, I gravitated to a new friend, John, who was at that time the president of the local Bass Society. John and his cohorts went on a tournament every week at different rivers in the Texas and neighboring states. He had a boat that could skim the surface of the water at three o'clock in the morning when the tournament started. The driver side, which he normally occupied, had a windshield that protected him against the onslaught of the cold breeze as he ripped through his chosen and favorite fishing spot. The passenger side where he had me assigned did not have any windshield, which made my face distorted by the cold eighty-mile-per-hour wind as we made through the fishing hole. On many occasions, we made the bragging rights, having reeled in the live and heaviest haul of the day, except one day when a big eight-pound bass was released into the water after the weighing and then caught in no time by a six-year-old on the opposite bank with a stick pole. His shriek of having landed a gargantuan fish was easily heard by everyone on the club. My spirit sagged, but I was eventually happy. It must have been the tyke's first catch of the day even though it was late in the afternoon.

Thomas Scott and Ernest Hemingway wrote about fishing and how it really was to them. I think they were men who relished the pleasure of the sport but occasionally brought home some of their picks. Aside from my friend John, who did it as a sport, a catch-and-release man who invited me to many of his trips outside the confines of Texas, luring me with big catches in hidden lakes and rivers in Mexico, the Amazon River in South America, in the pristine and wild inland waters of New York, and everywhere else, I did not always succumb to his ministrations. I went on my own, with some few friends, at some rivers and lakes in Colorado, New Mexico, even in Georgia and Rhode Island, always lugging my gear consisting of rod, reel, line, and baited hooks. It was not always as productive as I wanted it to be, especially when I was always on the lookout for that bear I bumped and almost ran over as I was on my way to a lake up in the mountain. It was also keeping an eye for the park ranger, who could cite you for using a natural lure when artificial bait was excruciatingly posted around the lake perimeter.

The thought of going back to the ocean to fish did not appeal to me after the disastrous experience in Sheepshead Bay, until I met Manny in one of the annual meetings of our surgical society. He was a sportsman extraordinaire: he traveled all around the world, hunting and fishing. He knew which season was best or optimum for every sport. He was also an accomplished neurosurgeon who yearly was involved in not only the pursuit of his passions but also his zeal of conducting and organizing yearly surgical missions to Third World countries.

He went to southeastern Alaska every summer to fish with one or two friends. One day, he asked me to join him together with another acquaintance. Five-member group from different parts of the country would meet at Sea Tac airport, fly to Ketchikan, and take a small plane parked in a galley of water. The bush pilot who looked like he had just graduated from high school prowled the small runway with coffee cup in his hand. I always lied about how much I weighed, but I was obliged to tell the receptionist of the small plane the truth, lest the plane would be overloaded and could not take off the ground for the one hour and fifteen minutes flight to the small house situated in the folds of the mountain and the Pacific Ocean. Rick and his common-law wife Cathy would always meet us at their house perched on the water, together with whatever packing necessities were required for the fishing camp they have been running for a number of years. Rick was a retired Coast Guard captain and knew his way around with his fishing boat, navigating and bringing his fishermen-guests to the Alaskan waters of the Pacific Ocean where, the depth finder in his boat would tell whether salmon, halibut, sea bass, or some other denizens of the sea were there to be had with appropriate lines and bait. The sea was manageable; the fishing boat, after a number of years, was replaced with a new one, was comfortable, except on the third year, when I prayed so hard for the second time in my lifetime. (The first time I am not allowed to tell, lest someone I know will not forgive me.) The water in the ocean was glassy and calm when suddenly, a gust of wind and rain came, lifting the boat two to three feet off the surface. This continued for an hour. I thought though Rick was cool as a cucumber. I wondered whether he always acted this way after many years of being at sea. He even joked while we were seated in the cabin white-knuckled that if we went any further, we would wind up in the Sea of Japan. Finally, after an hour, the sea was calm again. Home was where we decided to go, cut and freeze what we had that day.

We always got home after six to seven days, met by another and separate bush plane for our frozen load of salmon, halibut, sea bass, and other demersal fish for each of our destinations. Of course, for me, whatever poundage I brought home never lasted long. Extended hands were always around, knowing where I had been and demanding their share of the loot.

This continued yearly for nine years, until Manny passed away. Though he was subjected to pain in his remaining years, he always, up to the last minute, wanted to go to Alaska for fishing again.

I have not gone fishing since four years ago. It has remained an inviolable part of me, however, that every time I see a body of salt water or fresh water, the impulse of having the pole, line, reel, bait, and sinker overwhelms me.

For those engaged in commercial fishing who thought at one time that the resources in our rivers and our seas remain inexhaustible, the fact is the population of fish is really on the decline. While no official comprehensive statistics exist on the resources of the sea, those individual nations who have them say so. Indiscriminate fishing, overfishing, pollution, and not knowing fish culture, contribute to the natural catastrophe.

I will invite you, though, the next time I go fishing, if there are still fish left around.

> *Bragging may not bring happiness, but no man having caught a large fish goes home through an alley.*
>
> *Unknown*

Golf

Every time I watched the professional golfers at a PGA tournament on TV, I marvel how easy and relaxed their swing is, whether it is with a driver, an iron, a sand wedge or a putter. Most of the time the ball lands on the fairways and on the green. Seldom does it go under a tree or in the bush. And if it did, they always direct the errant shot to where the ball generally should be—in the cup. It can result in a par or even a birdie. Seldom a bogey. The trajectory of the shots can be followed with tracers, one of the many amazing advances in coverage of this challenging game. I have from the very beginning I picked up a golf club in my adult life that I would never be close to these guys, that the talent that I have about the game is so miniscule and would remain stuck unchanged in an abysmal handicap. After all, these pros have been swinging their clubs and learning the fundamentals of the game the moment they could stand up from infancy, on top of which as they advance in years and their abilities, have high-priced coaches who minister to correct every flaw they find in their game. In other words, I had and still do believe that the game was always for those who can afford the luxury of a country club that has a golf pro and a golf clubhouse among its many amenities.

It has been said that the most important business transactions in the present day are conducted not in the boardrooms of big corporations but in the fairways and greens of a golf course. Hearing this newfound aphorism did not make me a believer until one day in a hotel lobby, I met Danny Fabito. He was a vascular and laparoscopic surgeon from St. Louis, Missouri. He and I were attending the annual meeting and surgical symposium of a surgical society in which he was very active and at one time was its president. I had joined the society recently at that time and part of the four-day event included a golf game. Nonchalantly he asked if I was joining the golf outing, to which I answered no. He said that if I wanted to be a president of the society in the future, I needed to learn golf and join the group. Knowing my secret ambition to be one day become the president of the society after climbing up the ropes of becoming one, I took his admonition. After all, he came from the same town back home across the pond and his younger brother was a high school classmate of mine.

Back in Texas, I enrolled in a golf school, a veritable bastion of learning the game. I understand former Ben Crenshaw, a Masters champion was a student at the Harvey Penick Golf Academy, which made me more enthusiastic in joining the more than twenty-thousand former habitués despite the two-week sacrifice it inflicted on my surgical practice. All because of what I heard from Danny and the answer it might bring to my presidential ambition.

But it did turn out to be a lesson for me, learning about the history and intricacies of the game, its sizable part in the US economy, and most of all, as somebody steeped in anything related to health, the belief that golfers live five years longer than the average person. If anything, this was the most singular reason everyone should engage in this outdoor sport.

Learning the basics of the game, the eighteen holes in the course, the average distance—the fairways—between the starting point called the tee and the other end marked by a flag called the cup on a smooth surface called the putting green, was more than the chapters in a physics or mathematics book, both subjects that brought my grades down from a magna to cum laude. It is about hitting, spinning the ball, and the loft by an iron or a driver. I learned that to be a good golfer, one had to be proficient in the four points of the game: ball striking, short game, mental aspect and course management, and finally physical conditioning. To this day, I have abandoned all except the physical aspect—hopefully hitting the ball from the tee box and driving it for a short distance to the fairways.

What equipment to use and which would I proudly bring to the course to show a motley of golf addicts, I had to know. For instance, a standard set of clubs, the maximum I needed to carry was fourteen, numbers 1–5 called woods and 9–14 called irons. Utility and specialty clubs including the sand wedge, pitching wedge and the putters are different. I noted though that golfers who were of longstanding nature, carried less than the clubs I mentioned. I am not sure if this also applied to people like me, who have given up on which clubs to use despite having played the game ad infinitum.

Which made me think about Romy. He was an occasional once-in-an era golf mate, who did not care about my attempts at hits and strikes, except for his and knowledge about the game. He and I were neighbors, a few feet separated our doorsteps. And we were on the other side of the first tee box, separated by a four-foot fence that showed us every time we looked, who among the population of the town were teeing off. The golf pro at the clubhouse was a patient of his, and for someone like me, a neophyte of the game, took advantage of Romy's connections and the surreptitious times and discounted green fees, not to mention the free lessons or tips he gave him in exchange for the same the next time his follow-up appointment with Romy came up. Romy was always quick to point out that his drives, hooks, or slices were not the result of his mechanics gone awry but the fault of the equipment he used. I always expected that the next time we hit the course, he came up with a new club to rescue his shanks and erratic ball, which he did. The number I played with him was as scarce as Halley's comet visiting Earth. It became even scarcer when he moved out of town to take up better opportunities associated with his profession. But it did not matter to me because I never expected to be as good as he was, even better than those pros sometimes I watched on television when football season was over.

I had the selfish idea that I took up the game so that I could be president of a society one day. I developed the courage and temerity to join the annual golf tournament that the society had as part of its membership and fellowship affair. I knew I wouldn't measure up to those that made the game as part of their sports routine. I never made it close to the scores or their handicaps, though out of desperation or luck, I was closest to the pin on a par 3 hole one time. On one occasion, I even went onstage to accept the sports award I did not expect I would receive—for the most numbers of balls lost. But I finally became one day, the president of the surgical society, the first to have been elected for two terms, all because of Danny and him telling me to be a golfer.

I have since retired from active surgical practice four years ago. I do not consider myself a golfer, but I joined a group that meets and plays every week at different courses where it can negotiate the price of a green fee. Not serious and an occasional at the game, I have the highest handicap in every course we play, which makes me always a threat to everyone with the low handicap subtracted from the gross score for a low net. On a few occasions, I have won the eighteen- to twenty-dollar prize competition money. It is the obvious but maybe malevolent reason I asked and told our club president not to alter my high handicap.

One day, Ben was in our foursome following another group on a golf course in New Mexico. One of the golfers ahead of us teed off, and the ball went to a place he was not happy about. He shouted a curse word that was audible to most of us. Ben, who proudly was showing an old driver made of persimmon earlier, heard the curse word and commented how it was that people said profane words when it was only a game. He teed off when his turn came, and his ball hooked or sliced so that he was not able to find it. Out of disgust, he rammed his driver, broke it into pieces, and uttered the four-letter word that I did not expect would come from this man's mouth. Meekly, I patted him on the shoulder and said, "It is only a game."

To me, golf is only a game. I have already been a president of the surgical society. If it makes me live five years longer, I will continue to take it.

Golf is the closest game we call life. You get bad breaks from good shots; you get good breaks from bad shots—but you have to play the ball where it lies.

—Bobby Jones, American golfer, four-time winner of US Open

The most important shot in golf is the next one.

—Ben Hogan, American golfer, winner of nine major championships including US Open, Masters, and PGA

Cruising

I am not done with cruises yet. Cruising has provided me with what the rest of the world looks like, not through the prism of dreams as I had once but through the eyes of someone who, taking advantage of a shrinking universe, can now see the reaches of the globe, from north to south and east to west. It is also the most economical and cheapest, considering that the depth of my purse can be easily fathomed with half the length of my hands. The sleeping quarters (though not the bedroom of our small house), the entertainment on board the ship, the different islands and places the cruise line drops its anchor are adventures waiting to be explored. But what is more enticing to a wanderer like me is the variety of food that I need not prepare or cook. It is all for the taking, at scheduled dinners, at every nook in the ship. I had to weigh myself before I got on board, to see how much weight I inevitably gained when the cruise ended. And I can easily get away from the table without the recourse of cleaning it up or washing the platter and the silverware. That is the good life as I could imagine growing up.

I have been to the countries of the West. I have been to the islands and the kingdoms of the East. On all the places I have been to, I have done it with all modes of transportation, skimming across the water or the skies. Lucky that advances in technology are available now than the horse-and-buggy days of the past. I could only imagine how the travails of travel, moving from one place to another had been to those courageous enough to undertake the experience.

The land called holy, where the confluence of religions and beliefs of most the whole world exists after thousands of years, baffles me. Why were the three major religions founded in a small piece of land where up to now, the Catholics, together with the Orthodox Christians, the Jews, and Muslims claim to have sprouted, guarding every relic that stands for the faith they all believe in? And all bow before the same God they have appended different names to. If these religions originated from a small swath of land, could it be because many years ago, the prophets and the disciples were limited by horses and donkeys and dinghies in propagating their beliefs and travels like we know now did not exist two thousand years ago? I belong to one of the churches that has more than a billion followers, although I respect the other faiths. Did Jesus really walk on water? Because I tried and got submerged up to my waist in the process. Or does the Wailing Wall miraculously bring to reality the wishes left behind in small widgets inserted through its crevices? How about the Golden Dome that is so holy to Islam—is it where Mohammed ascended to heaven?

On the eastern side of the globe, where monolithic atheism, ascetic monks, beliefs in different deities pervaded the population and provided me with what I have read and learned from travelogues. Angkor Wat, the Eternal City and Tiananmen Square, the Chuchi trail and all the temples erected in the name of all the deities have brought me close to history and what it means to be a part of the past.

The big cruise lines that ferry thousands of travelers every year to different parts of the Caribbean and the Mediterranean, as well as to the far ends of Tawi-Tawi and the islands of the South Pacific, are floating hotels that cater to those who have disposable time and income for the luxury of exploring the oceans and the seas. Others like me are forced to have this option of average citizens for an affordable but fascinating vacations. Recently, I have found that river cruises are more suitable for my tastes than boarding an upscale mega cruise line. I have been to many of them, East and West, and relished the idea of having a calmer trip through the locks in a river that meanders its way to different cities, historical sites, and sundrenched spots of a particular country. The limited number of accommodations and the chance of knowing everyone on board from different parts of the globe have become appealing. I have seen the birthplace of Mozart, of Padre Pio, the palaces where the kings and queens wallow in comfort and luxury, noticing the yoke of subservient subjects. And what was fascinating was to know that an emperor or a king could have as many concubines as one's stamina allowed. Do that today and face walls on four sides from a felony called polygamy. I hear that it does not deter others though from secretly engaging in this felonious activity.

It has been a learning experience with many lecturers on every river port, giving a presentation that enriched my shrunken cortex and amygdala with the culture and history of the places river cruise visited.

Seeing these faraway places and not knowing what my own backyard looks like makes me feel guilty. You see, I grew up in a small clustered community and was deprived economically of any means of going to what is called a tourist haven in my old country. Being a lot older and saving enough, I have gone to places I have read and dreamed of as a child; cruising and traveling have moved me to the exotic and foreign historical destinations, even up to now.

But lately, my bucket lists have included seeing and experiencing my own backyard before my knees and my legs begin to give up on me. If the latter happens, I might need someone to hold me up if I continue with my cruising.

> *Twenty years from now you will be more disappointed by the things you didn't do than by the ones you did do. So throw off the bowlines, sail away from the safe harbor. Catch the winds in your sails. Explore. Dream. Discover.*
>
> —Mark Twain, American writer and author

Driving

One of the records I am so proud of but never talked or discussed about is my driving, which for many years contained only a smidgen of raps that I almost don't remember exist, until about four years ago. I pulled out the old red Mercedes-Benz 560 SL 1988 from the garage where it has always hibernated since I bought it from a dealership the year it came out. It was to start its engine for an occasional drive for a few gallons to a station where the cost is a few cents cheaper than the prevailing rates in the vicinity. I was on the left side, crawling into a two-lane road down a hill at 30 mph where it said 25 mph. I was overtaken by other vehicles on the faster lane, obviously speeding more than the 30 miles per hour clip I pushed my speedometer on. I do not mean to justify my five-mile transgression. Out from his perch on a hill, a motorcycle cop swooped down, turned on his siren and his red, white, and blue lights, and told me to pull over. I did, aware that those motorists passing by knew I committed a violation that, if not for the color of my car, they would not have escaped the violation I was to be charged with. As the cop checked on me as to whether I was a serial rapist or an alien pervert enough to have other intrastate or out-of-state criminal records, while sitting astride his motorcycle with his computer. It dawned on me what an old friend told me: that these uniformed enforcers of the traffic laws were given a number of violators they have to write each period, that as measure of their efficiency and subsequent promotion to driving a police car of their own, they have to fulfill. I realized that it was the end of the month.

Cops or troopers somehow always greet whomever they pull over to the side of the street with what I think they were told in the law enforcement school or academy. I was greeted with the perfunctory "Good morning" by an officer who sidled up on the driver's side, his right hand resting on his holstered gun like I was about to pull out an IED and discharge it in his face. My only question was that there were other vehicles on the faster side of the road than I was and why he specifically picked me. I did not for a moment believe he answered my question when he said that he had been watching me singularly up the hill. He asked if there was any reason I was in a hurry that I had to push down on the pedal. One thing that I was told by a trooper-friend sometime back in another state was that in his academy years, they were told a hundred or so excuses or reasons motorists give when pulled over. I did not offer any explanation, handed my license and all the documents needed by the officer, who did not give me a warning but a ticket that I had to bring in to the traffic court in a week. Shortly before I proceeded to the gas station, another red car was pulled over in front of me by another cop. Red was not the color of that day.

There was a law firm that specialized in appearing or more commonly, as I found out, parlayed its municipal court connections in erasing traffic violations from your traffic rap sheet. It emblazoned itself on a TV commercial showing the pink building where the office was and blaring with a picture of a cop whose eye shades and hat covered much of his face. Wanting to preserve the sanctity of my driving record and avoid the appearance before a court, arguing my side of the story, I fell for the charges of the law firm's effort as against the cost imposed by the court and the added stain my record would suffer should my plea be dismissed. I was not informed that I had to take the state's driving education program and be tested. It took me three weeks to have it, couldn't hurry up even if I thought I answered the questions ahead of the mandated time allotted to give the response and finish the course at an earlier time. I was also to take a final exam and pass it to the clerk at the office, who informed me that he was from the state I came from and that he was only employed there for a short period of time. In the end, I am glad I took the course because I got reminded of the many things I see on the road that I don't pay any attention to what they mean. I also passed the requisite tests, and to record it for posterity and my subsequent heirs, I had pictures with my diploma, taken outside the office with its pink paint and the cop with oversized sunglasses. My traffic ticket was erased after the greater cost and time than I anticipated. By the way, I never saw or met the lawyer whose name was attached to the firm.

Driving is an exhilarating activity, especially if one drives down a wide, open highway in a brand-new sports car such as when I leased a low-slung red (I always have an eye for something red) NSX many years ago. I drove it from a showroom 300 miles from where I lived. Along the interstate, everyone I passed by looked at the car and me as if there was a blur and a passing fancy. My brother Jim, who drove the car one day, said I was crazy not to hold on to it once I had to return it after the lease period and after the low mileage in three years I registered on its speedometer. But there is inherently an appeal to one's vanity about a car made to run beautifully at 160–200 miles per hour when the limit is set to 55, later to 70 miles per hour. It is always game to push down on the floor the pedal and then pull it up and let go when one sees behind the telltale lights of a patrol car. The sports car I am talking about also had the state-of-the-art sound system which becomes uselessly muted and obliterated by the road noise generated when I play the cat-and-mouse game, tearing the road at a speed that was more than what the limit allowed.

I have been driving an eight-cylinder workhorse, a twenty-eight-year-old albatross with nearly 200,000 miles on its worn-out engine block. I have not tried the safety features of new vehicles such as the blind spot detection, lane departure warning, rear view camera, safety exit assist, or the automatic emerging brake. I am only limited by the airbags and the safety belts. But I have not had traffic ticket with it. Someday, I might be tempted to drive a new car.

As for the red car, I still have it in the garage.

> *You just have to keep driving down the road. It's going to bend and curve and you will speed and slow down, but the road keeps going.*
>
> *Ellen DeGeneres, American TV host*

Dancing

There are a couple of reality shows I usually watch whenever I watch television, which is more often than not. The format was all the same when the series started in 2005, and it is now on its twenty-seventh season. The celebrity is usually paired with a professional dancer, twelve or thirteen pairs in all, to dance to a specific routine each week. The celebrities—some well-known and others I have not heard of, and neither are some pollsters from Nielsen—are paired with professional dancers who were unknown until they climbed their way to become regulars in the show. The celebrities, a motley crowd of musicians, singers, football players, race-car drivers, movie actors whose luster during their heydays was as bright as the costumes they are fitted weekly have their careers at times resurrected by an appearance on the show. The panel of judges remains unchanged except on a few occasions when a substitute judge was called to pinch-hit for someone because of earlier commitments. There have been several short- and long-term hosts over the thirteen-year period that it has been a staple on the home screen, the last nine episodes co-hosted by Erin Andrews, she of the sports-announcer fame, who was at one time the subject of a peeping Tom's folly. The only permanent host of the show is Tom Bergeron, who was observed to have a head of black hair at the beginning but now has strands of gray atop his pate. He hauls the contestant before the panel of judges for them to obtain their scores for the night. The pair that is not eliminated and is left standing and has a multitude of 10s at the end of the competition wins the Mirror Ball trophy, which I suppose is less of an adornment than the Oscar statuette on a fireplace mantel that is covered that night with the winning pair's confetti dropped from the ceiling. For those that surf the television channels for other programs and don't know what I am talking about, it is called *Dancing with the Stars*.

Ever since I was able to stand on my own two feet, I always envisioned myself growing up with terpsichorean powers developed during formative years. In the small village where I grew up, I tried to attend almost every night festivity where I could watch a pair attempt a version of a slow dance at the expense of homework that I needed to finish for a class the following morning. The shyness of youth, the presumed unimportance of being young in age, and inability to take on a partner of the opposite sex made me a bystander rather than a performer. It was only once, during the end of a year that a girl I always pined for was anointed by my schoolteacher as a partner for a dance we were committed to a semblance of perfection in a daily after-school three- to four-week practice for an audience at the end commencement exercise. It was the only time I was able to shake a leg for a dance I have longed for.

But the dance that I was most interested as I became of age is the Argentine tango. I watched many times how a blind Lieutenant Colonel Frank Slade, played by Al Pacino in the film *Scent of a Woman*, was able to convey the incredible rhythm of an art form. Not that the exuberance of salsa or rhumba or samba was lost on me, but the contorted staccato of the tango with the long legs of the lady wrapped around the waist of the well-proportioned physique of the partner became a controlling force so hard to pull from. In my years in Texas, I enrolled in a dance studio in faraway Florida, where a Hispanic couple ostensibly dance instructors sent me periodically written materials and CDs detailing dance moves and steps I was to practice for the dance in which I was going to be an expert or connoisseur in the future. On the days that I was off and my wife was on call, the solitary confinement of the bedroom became a dancing hall when I plugged in the CD player and started imitating the step-by-step instructions on a video provided by my two faraway dance instructors. The day would come, I thought, when I would be able to surprise my friends the moment my partner and I trod to the dance floor and showed them what I had been secretly engaged in. Or when my hands would be protectively holding the curves of a partner dripping from her tight costume. After many months and innumerable attempts at being a polished figure in a dance floor, I came, however, to the inevitable conclusion that my leaden feet were not meant to be supple and light to skim the hall like the druids that the professional dancers were. The agony of defeat and the reality after all of just being a surgeon descended on me like a brick hurled into my face. The couple from Florida have not given up, however, their hopes that someday they could still whip me into the mold I thought I would be four decades ago. They still keep sending me an invitation to reconnect an association I have given up many years ago. I don't know if they are still alive.

The history and the origin of dance is as old as the existence of man (and woman). From its early beginning to its passage into the present, the transition has always been an expression of human thoughts and emotion, of civilization detailed by the diversity of cultures in every society. One can point to an era and the ethnic origin of or energy of a rhythm by the nature of a dance. The dance popular during the sixteenth century, the Elizabethan dance of courtly artisans was a hybrid of what we know as line dancing and square dance with its measured cadence. It was a way of exercise and socialization among the crowd. The nineteenth century showed us the introduction of the waltz popularized by the music of Johann Strauss. The waltz, which remains today the gold standard of ballroom dancing and started during the Renaissance period, was, however, supplanted by a different form of waltz called the Viennese waltz, first performed by the Italians to synchronize with a much faster 180 beats per minute. Today there are so many forms of dances, some traditional, others variations and improvisations of the old and the new, the amalgamation called modern, its component dynamics developed over the years. India has several officially recognized dances; China has the dragon dance, Cuba is noted for its salsa,

Russia its ballet, and Japan, the kabuki. Tango, originally the "dance of the underprivileged," had its beginning in Buenos Aires and in Montevideo, Uruguay. South America had the energetic and captivating Latin dances that are always fascinating and sensual. One can recognize easily those dance styles emanating from African origin, as with the newer forms of disco, line, hip-hop, breakdance, funk, moonwalk and the more sedate swing and the handclaps of flamenco.

I have since given up the idea that I will be a hoofer extraordinaire. It was once an imagination I wanted to be real but remained beyond my grasp and limited ability. So now, when I find my way to the dance floor—which is rare—with my wife, who dances better than me, I am made aware that I do not possess the heavy and complex moves demanded by the jive or the boogie. I just move to the beat of the music, knowing that I will never be chosen as a celebrity partnering with someone as pretty as Lindsey Arnold or Sharma Burgess.

This much I can be sure of, though: I won't be dancing all the way to the bank.

There is nothing impossible to him who will try.

Alexander the Great

Collecting

Alexandrina Victoria, who is most commonly known as Queen Victoria, was the queen of the United Kingdom of Great Britain and Ireland from May 1837 to January 1901 who was crowned when she was only eighteen years of age. Her reign of sixty-three years and seven months was longer than any of her predecessors' and was characterized by cultural, political, scientific, and military expansion of the British Empire, with her taking the additional title of Empress of India in 1876. The period was known as the Victorian era. Despite all the celebration and jubilees that marked the years of her golden rule, the British postal rates were noted to be "high, complex, and anomalous." The recipient paid for the mail based on the distance travelled, the cost of the sheet and the weight of the letter delivered. In an effort to relieve this burden to the general public, the concept of the adhesive stamp was proposed and developed during her reign. It featured the profile of Queen Victoria, attached to the envelope of a letter, delivered at a flat rate of one penny regardless of the distance. It is the only postage stamp in the world that does not indicate the country from which it originated; the image of its monarch tells it all. The stamp was issued for sale on May 6, 1840, and lasted for less than a year. Abuses included its reuse after the red cancellation mark on its black design was easily erased and removed by people determined to reuse it despite the Treasury's steps to safeguard this postal innovation. During its print run, 286,700 sheets were printed, which had 68,808,000 stamps called Penny Black. Some still remain and are usable as many were saved. Some are readily available to stamp collectors. In 1972, I became a Penny Black collector, purchasing a postmarked British stamp for $200 after making sure it was not a counterfeit. I still have it and don't have any idea whether its value has gone up or down.

The Penny Black started me on collecting stamps. It started with the gleaming surface of 22-carat golden replicas of United States stamps issued by the Postal Commemorative Society. The golden replicas were pasted on a 2" × 2" maroon-colored bed, with an envelope attached that had my name and address and a historical description of whatever the commemorative stamp was all about, whether the year of Delaware's statehood, T. S. Elliott's literary series, or a Navajo's tribal chief's art. First Day Covers from Around the World brought stamps detailing plant life in Transkei, ocean shells in Djibouti, and the tenth annual Independence Day on October 1980 in Fiji added to the collection carefully encased in an ornately designed binder. A friend of Croatian descent and president of the local philatelic society invited me to be a member and started giving me a stamp collection from his forebears' native country, adding to the burgeoning collection that I intended to limit myself to. But the more promises I made to myself about the restraints I needed to impose on my collecting paraphernalia that I laid my eyes on, the more of these resolutions fell by the wayside.

Though I never won any match or tournament, I was once the president of a chess club during my undergraduate years at the university. I was made the president, I think, because there was nobody among the membership who was willing to come forward and organize the events of the club. Therefore, chess sets became part of what I collected later in my life. I still have many of them stashed away in some unopened boxes, though at one time, the collection was prominently displayed in several nooks of the house we moved from. Collecting items and storing them in the order that they were issued became a compulsion, especially as I had other activities I needed to accommodate with my time. It never was considered as hoarding to add to or pad my collection; hoarding was more of storing anything and everything, regardless of its usefulness or value until the place on which it is accumulated becomes a site filled with garbage. Besides, I never considered myself psychologically disturbed, which most hoarders are.

A few years ago, I pulled my two children into the three storage areas I was renting. I also showed what collections my wife and I had in our house, knowing that sometime in a not-too-distant future, both inevitably will inherit any earthly possessions we patiently collected. Dismay at the miniscule enthusiasm and response that nowadays children have of their parents' material resources and the label of "dust collector" on the collections, especially the figurines that adorn the étagères and cabinets in the living room, gave me the notion that collecting is a passion that we the aging and the old have to give up. I have since stopped my collection of stamps, chess sets, and the like.

There is a reality show that debuted in 2010. It still runs every week today, with Mike Wolfe and Frank Fritz of *American Pickers* going across the continental United States and searching for memorabilia generated by Danielle Colby from Fritz's office. Driving earlier a Mercedes pickup, now a Ford Transit on which their outfit Antique Archaeology is proudly emblazoned, both entrepreneurs collect and buy old picks and haul them back to their stores and ultimately sell them, Fritz at his own shop and his website. With viewers in the millions, it probably will continue with its weekly episodes for many more seasons and will be syndicated long after it is gone.

There is a chance that if Mike and Frank will get tired of their popular gig, I may take over, from collecting and going to old shops and museums, buying and selling. I just need to find someone like Danielle to direct me to out-of-the-way towns or places.

> *Most of those who make collections of verse or epigram are like men eating cherries or oysters: they choose out the best at first, and end by eating all.*
>
> *Nicolas Chamfort, a French writer and a Mason*

Cooking

I am always fascinated by how much the gastronomic landscape has become a prominent field lately. It has evolved into a big industry, with culinary schools achieving at times an entrance competition ordinarily seen in some Ivy League institutions of higher learning and has made chefs into well-known celebrities bigger than what I think they originally intended to be. Dining in fancy restaurants and savoring the recipes and concoctions of those who we see on TV has become a luxury to some and a sign of prestige to many. I suppose the saying "The way to a woman's heart is through her stomach" has become passé these days when defining nouvelle cuisine has become gender neutral. Julia Child, who was widely known to have "made" public television with her "French show," popularized culinary art with her black-and-white show, 200 episodes of them, the last of which, I recall, was aired in 1972. While she was known by her assistants and employees for her sense of organization, little was known for her covering up her flubs and slips such as dropping a potato pancake into the counter, scooping it back into the skillet because "nobody is looking." The spilled liquids and the famous episode where she tried to use several knives carving up a roast suckling pig is something one does not see in today's Food Network cooking shows.

Today, cooking is an art form. The origin of cooking, however, is obscure, and no single individual can definitely pinpoint where it originated. Anthropologists and archaeologists claim that it began

250,000 to 300,000 years ago when burnt animal bones and flints were found across Europe and the Middle East. The primitive humans may have accidentally savored the meat of a beast killed in a forest fire and discovered that it was easier to chew and digest than when it was eaten raw. Other finds indicate that our human ancestors started cooking two million years ago, providing evidence that plant ashes and burnt bone were the result of fire during those early times. Man found that cooking predigests food, therefore use less energy to process or break it down inside the body.

Cooks are the purveyors of food. Fundamentally, cooking is a skillset and is a profession where individuals prepare the food in a variety of ways for consumption. It is now a highly regarded career where cooks are sometimes referred to as chefs, although the terms in the culinary world are not interchangeable. To be a chef is to be someone who obtains a professional degree and prepares food in a professional setting, while a cook does not have to be necessarily so. The word *chef* originated in the nineteenth century and comes from the Latin word *caput* translated into "chief" in English. To demonstrate its importance and the high regard of being a chef, the serious ones wear white to signify cleanliness, a starched white hat called a toque, and an apron for hygienic and identification purposes. Seldom are these accoutrements worn by the modern-day chefs that prattle across a gleaming kitchen and apportioned ingredients of the recipes they are to make. Think of Bobby Flay or Guy Fieri, even Giada or Rachael Ray who come into their own TV shows dressed like they were going to a party where the dress code is as you come.

Nena prepared our daily meal for many years when the family was ensconced in Texas. Her recipes were all ethnic and parochial and were as good as those on cookbooks. Seldom did we dine out, cognizant that homemade cooking was touted as better than any other outside of the home. But over the long haul, however, she started cooking the recipes she saw on the Food Channel, and we were made to judge how well; the dishes she cooked were acceptable or as good as what the chef on TV's instructed. It did not rate a Michelin star as Emeril Lagasse, Gordon Ramsay, or Tilman Fertitta did with their cuisine translocated to their restaurants, but it did satisfy our palates. We left her with her husband when we moved to the place where my wife and I are now, though occasionally we call her for something we need for a certain taste to what we have on the stove, despite the many cookbooks arrayed in the kitchen.

Sometime ago while on a trip to Napa Valley, visiting the different vineyards and sampling the different wines distilled in their oak flasks, I attended a course offered by the Culinary Institute of America, one of the prestigious culinary schools in America. I watched as different professional chefs from several well-established restaurants and dining places demonstrated their skills churning out recipes and haute cuisine. Aside from visiting the herb garden from which they harvested the greens and the necessary condiments of their cooking and purchasing the sweatshirt and the chef garb that identified me as an attendee to CIA, I really did not remember anything I seriously committed to my culinary memory, until two years ago. Left to my own devices, having left Nena and her husband in Texas, and with nobody to cook or prepare our dinner, I assumed the change from being a surgeon to a "chef," much like my cardiologist friend who became adept at cooking as his newfound profession in exchange for the stethoscope and the different murmurs of the heart. On a trip to Lyon, France, I enrolled at Paul Bocuse's culinary school if only for a day. I was surprised that his school offered a bachelor's and master's degree in the culinary arts and the many years he obtained the three-star Michelin ratings for high quality and his innovative approach to cooking. I was instructed on how to make a *classique* salad, a nouvelle dish, how to tell a fresh from an old egg by how the yolk behaves when dropped into a cold water. The class was made to eat whatever they cooked. Having learned but a smidgen of French cuisine from one who is multi-awarded throughout his career, including the medal of Commandeur de la Legion d'honneur, I developed a liking for French food however much the sauce is all buttery. Paul Bocuse passed away at age ninety-one on January 20, 2018.

Cooking a dish or recipe involves a lot of artistry and imagination. It has been said that the appreciation engendered by a specific dish is not so much of how it tastes—as most taste is acquired—but of how it is presented on a plate. Decorated with flowers, powdered sugar, a calorie-laden sauce, in an ambience of opulent brassiere, a comfort food becomes an appetizing classic dish. No matter how exotic the cooking I have become familiar with, I have not lost the taste of the traditional recipes I learned from my mother. Maybe I will just give it a different name.

> *Cooking is like painting or writing a song. Just as there are only so many notes or colors, there are only so many flavors—it is how you combine them that sets you apart.*
>
> *Wolfgang Puck, famous chef and restaurateur*

Keeping Time

"A stitch in time saves nine." Whoever wrote this aphorism knows the importance of time. It has been man's preoccupation to have a way of measuring or defining segments of the night and day, in which the moon and the sun cause us to sleep or wake up. It was the reason why time was invented, and the many devices to measure it were created dating back to 1,500 BC when the Egyptians founded the shadow clock or sundial that measured the passage of hours within a day. Finding a more accurate way of measuring passage of time than looking at a shadow cast by a crossbar on a nonlinear rule led to a water clock invented by Ctesibius using a simple outflow of flow of water called a clepsydra, which was used by the ancient Greeks and the Romans. The sundials became more accurate though until the nineteenth century, when they remained a common and popular way of telling the time. Another way of telling time was the first hourglass or sand clock invented by a French monk called Liutprand in the eighth century AD. British archaeologists claim that man discovered time 8,000 BC when they excavated the Mesolithic monument in Scotland in 2004 and believe that this was the oldest calendar by ancient hunters and gatherers. Time is abstract; lost it can't be recovered, but the past can be considered a history.

We are all aware of the fact that everything in life is measured in terms of time and the questions that we all ask if we fall in line at the counter, at the cash register, flying or driving from point A to B, or for anything that demands a span of minutes or hours in our everyday life. We often fret and become irritable when it takes longer than we expect how long it would be before we reach the end of the line and be served or attended to. One has to look at the myriad of timepieces that everyone, from street sidewalk to the exclusive rooms of jewelry boutiques, sells as their wares, ranging from the price of a fake to the value of the real in an effort to adorn our wrists. These are the watches, originally invented in 1923 by a British watch repairer John Harwood, that we indulge in to keep us constantly aware that time is a bubble, a valuable commodity that, once lost, can never be recovered. The multiple and available sounds we set on our wall and pendulum clocks, the hourly toll from a belfry announcing the time of day always announce an opportunity for us never to squander our mornings, afternoons, and evenings but use them in the best possible way. Men and women who utilize their time purposefully have always been successful. Being punctual should be the principle we follow, as it avoids inconvenience in a life that, as we men and women know, has finite years to be lived. Time brings opportunity, which properly taken advantage of is an ingredient of achievement.

To suggest that being a stickler for time has brought me success in life might be a stretch. But I have always tried to keep pace with what I schedule for the day and not engage in thoughtless and purposeless activities. To have an unscheduled drop-in in the middle of a busy day, a sudden visit to a friend or relative that is not included in someone's calendar that particular week, or an unexpected event requiring a change of plans already made are distractions to orderly and invaluable moments in time. To bring up the value of always keeping abreast and on time has been like an order barked but not carried out or paid attention to by some of my relatives and friends. The command to be punctual, as time, like the tide, does not wait for anyone and does not behave in fits and starts, falls mostly on deaf ears.

It must have been this anatomical disregard that Pete, a friend of mine asked me one day if I could pick him up one afternoon for a conference we were to attend that started at a particular time. He was always lackadaisical about observing time and punctuality, and I was actually pleasantly surprised when he asked me to fetch him knowing that I was always obsessed with looking at my watch. He was true to form because when I appeared at his doorstep, he was not even dressed up. I had to wait for him, with all the usual explanations he had to muster to justify not being prepared for the hour-long trip. We sat in the last row, half an hour late. I did not even recall the subject matter that we were supposed to hear that afternoon, although our friendship and all the civility involved did not result in me picking him up again at another time.

Sir Sandford Fleming, Canada's foremost construction engineer and inventor who developed the system of standard time as we know it, still in use today, might not be able to define what time exactly means but did know how valuable it is, each second and minute leaving us a concrete footprint we all need to trace back. Determined as I am to impress its value, I have given up sometimes to impose this concept on most people and friends I know about horology, the evolution and the importance of time.

> *Time is like a river. You cannot touch the same water twice because the flow that has passed will never pass again. Enjoy every moment in life.*
>
> *—Inspirational quote*
>
> *Time is free, but it is priceless. You can't own it but you can use it. You can't keep it, but you can spend it. Once you have lost it, you can never get it back.*
>
> *—Harvey Mackay, New York Times best-selling author and syndicated columnist*

Bird-Watching

My introduction to bird-watching was almost apocryphal, except that when I moved from the big metropolis known as New York to a small county town in West Texas, I met Frank. He was a political kingmaker in the county who, among other things, urged me to run for an office of which for twenty-four years until I voluntarily hung up my gloves, I did not face any opposition during election time. He also had an insurance company that bore his name, and I would think at that time he had almost everyone and every office in the county under his insured list. He invited me to his house one day after coming in from Dallas to retrieve his prized possession, a Granget sculpture of a bird, for which he paid an inordinate sum. I did not know that among his civic involvement in the community, he was also an enthusiastic birder who was instrumental in having a small aviary incorporated in the small city park when it was renovated. To impress him, I ordered a smaller Gunther Granget gold-plated bronze of two birds in flight, which I still have in our living room. He asked me to join his group for planned bird-watching trip locally in the corners of the Texas Panhandle, where he was familiar with the seasons during which specific flurries appear or return and the plumage that a red robin or a cardinal flaunts. That started my interest in this activity, which is considered a sport to millions of enthusiasts around the globe. Although I was not as active as Frank was in pursuing the recreation, I nevertheless joined a few groups of watchers whenever they scheduled a local trip. To look the part in this newfound hobby, I even invested in necessary equipment such as binoculars that constantly hung from my neck during these activities, and cameras to record for the life list on which I had to write the species I saw that day. I even purchased the field guide *Birds of North America* by Robbins, Bruun, and Zim to be able to identify over 800 species of birds and 100 more in other parts of the country. I did not go out and participate in traveling to other parts of the country, much less to other countries, chasing the other 10,000 types and species of birds.

Bird-watching or birding is a popular hobby or sport watching birds in their natural habitat. In North America, a birder, who is someone who has taken up the sport, is more often called a chaser. A twitcher is a name reserved for those that travel long distances to see a rare bird in its environment. There are more than 60 million American bird-watchers who spend thousands of dollars for the equipment, travel, transportation, lodging, educational and informational materials, generating the industry more than $36 billion a year in revenues. Bird-watchers are interested to know about the different bird species' appearance, behavior, location, and how they feed and survive. What formation or pattern the flock of birds assume while flying the skies and which one among them leads during the flight; what causes them to migrate and move to hundreds or thousands of miles away from their natural habitat, only to return to their place of origin at some point in a year are some of the questions bird-watchers incessantly ask. *National Geographic*, in its January 2018 issue, devoted much of its pages to birds and why they matter. From the great hornbill in Southeast Asia, to the ringed teal in South America, the black-throated magpie-jay in Mexico, or Kirtland's warbler in Michigan, the beauty and the idiosyncrasies of different birds in the planet are brought to the attention and focus by people who consider themselves bird-watchers and bird lovers, which is what brought the creation of the National Audubon Society, incorporated in 1905 as a nonprofit organization for the purpose of organizing bird-watching field trips but more importantly for its conservation-related activities in preserving healthy ecosystems. Named after James Audubon, a

French-American naturalist and ornithologist who, with his *Birds of America* book in 1827, painted and described birds of North America, the society has 500 chapters in the US with partners in diverse communities worldwide.

I am not totally sure whether a retired internist-gastroenterologist and his nurse-wife friends of ours were members of the National Audubon Society. But before and since their retirement, they always sent us a list and some of the pictures of the birds they had seen for the first time and the many birds they have identified in their bird-watching trips in the different parts of the country and around the world. I don't have the strong drive to the element of surprise and adventure they have developed, but I have not turned my back on what Frank had me interested in the first time he showed me what a roadrunner looked like. Although I have not actively looked for new birds in new sites and other countries, conservation centers, or other remote places I have been at, I nevertheless consider myself still a conservationist, avoiding hunting and abusing the nearly 321 species I have seen pictures of in the endangered list. At our house where we recently moved a few years ago, the backyard has been a sanctuary of birdhouses and bird feeders, making me one of the eight-eight percent of backyard birders. The waterfall installed has become a daily and hourly watering hole for different types of birds attracted by the sound of the coastal flow and the hanging feeders with sugar water a declared territory of the hummingbird every day.

Frank passed way several years ago. My gastroenterologist friend, after a bird-watching trip to Iceland, succumbed several months ago. It reminds me every day that bird-watching is not only about feathery friends but those that introduced you to them.

> *Birds teach us something very important: To whatever height you rise, you will finally come to the ground.*
>
> —*Mehmet Murat Ildan, Turkish contemporary writer and playwright*

Shopping

Daniel Patrick Moynihan, longest serving senator of New York, so far tied with Jacob Javits, famously said, "Everyone is entitled to their own opinion but they are not entitled to their own facts." Growing up and a resident at one time in his home state, I have followed the late sociologist, academic, diplomat, and political figure's meteoric rise; this native Oklahoman, humble as he was in my estimation, did not openly acknowledge his personal accomplishments over the course of his lifetime. But I have formulated, like he said, my own opinions about things and sets of facts, some of which are formed by personal observations and not necessarily derived through scientific and accepted conclusions. For example, I can tell the difference between a female and male, not only by their genotypes and phenotypes but by the way they behave when they shop. Besides, nowadays, with the emphasis on what one looks like, it is no longer kosher or important in determining what gender a shopper is. While this observation why I could tell easily why a female is distinctly different from a male shopper is a personal conclusion, I am inclined to believe that there are many who, like me, still tread through corridors of brick-and-mortar malls, accompanying their significant other who find themselves entitled to this fact.

Shopping has become a leisure activity to most people and not (like in older times and the Middle Ages) a chore for which women originally were responsible. In an earlier report, it was found that 80 percent of customers were women, who now view shopping as a pleasurable and recreational activity. The agora in ancient Greece and the forums of Rome are now replaced by malls, arcades, and department stores, attracting customers to these established centers of consumption. Harrods in London, Bloomingdale's and Saks in New York, Galeries Lafayette in France, and others opened in the mid-eighties and early nineties with attractive fronts, advertisements, fashions, and other exquisite goods, with restaurants and food stalls added as patronage haunts. The growth and expansion of the shopping malls have been fueled by a middle class with more discretionary income, the younger generation who have more disposable funds to spend, the developers of malls that cater to the retailers' and customers' idea of an enjoyable experience in shopping, and the media and marketing communication's ability to whet the consumer's temptations. It was no longer the worn-out "buy what you need" but "what you want" mentality, exacerbated by the ubiquitous promotions and sales advertised by stores.

During the period of what I call accumulation, my wife and I were enamored of shopping whenever we could, mostly on weekends and holidays we were off, going to centers and stores and bringing home wares, fashion accessories, and the like. We were by no means, however, considered shopaholics. It was on these trips where I observed that for a particular good that she wanted to purchase and found in one store, she would defer buying it, go to another store, hoping that it had the same or a similar article for a lower price, or wait until it was offered on a sale. This was not a onetime occasion but repeated so many times over the years that it annoyed me and made me conclude that all women were alike. After all, women buy 80 percent of everything that is on sale. Therein lies my assumption of a gendered fact of identification. For men like me, it was always knowing what we want, dashing into a store, and walking out in no time with whatever we wanted in our hands. These days, we look at things we have accumulated and wonder what mental experience we had that made us go shopping for what we want but really not what we need. Unloading some or all of what we now consider unnecessary items, a period now we call distribution to our children or potential heirs has not so far yielded the results we were expecting.

With the advent of the Internet and electronic commerce, a new way of shopping has emerged. Coupled with free delivery system, it now allows consumer to shop from home, ordering goods from catalogs, print media, television ads, etc. after evaluating, comparing, and looking at the price of a particular product. It is projected that in the year 2020, 49 percent or $252 billion in sales will result from online shopping, favored by 67 percent of millennials, who would rather utilize this medium than go to a mall or store. While the convenience of shopping online is apparent such as savings in time, beating the traffic or not staying in queue, not committing to impulse of buying immediately, the ease of buying in one place, or the 24-hour open online store availability, traditional shopping to most people still remains appealing. While the threat of the online shopping phenomenon has been steadily growing in the last two decades, it is not a death knell for in-store shopping.

Though we still find it pleasurable to touch the various products inside or indulge in examining merchandise and leaf through the pages of a book by strolling through the aisles of a department store, the newfound method of online shopping was not lost to us. Every now and then, I find at the doorstep a package from QVC or MSN, only to learn that she has taken to the TV and the Internet with the aid of her credit card to order or request UPS or FedEx deliver the merchandise. While I have become fully aware that there are disadvantages to online shopping, such as the stolen identity or credit card info, possibility of wrong or damaged merchandise from shipping, returning and then waiting for the right and undamaged product, these frustrations have not prevented me from trying and ultimately taking to utilizing this method of shopping, sometimes. I have ordered from different websites items for the best price available from various distributors and vendors or find products that I think will not be available at the brick-and-mortar shops close by. The difference between then and now is that whatever I buy, whether it be at a mall or online, I absolutely need it. The ring on a doorbell at a time when I expect the package to arrive is not a surprise event, like when I am not informed about a delivery I did not know or anticipate.

"Shop till you drop" is often an afterthought of a typology type known as recreational shoppers, who think of the activity as a form of leisure. Don't count me in this group. While I think of traditional shopping as it exists today and the new and still-evolving medium of online shopping as a pleasure, the activity is not only leisure but a necessary chore.

> *I always say shopping is cheaper than a psychiatrist.*
>
> *—Tammy Faye Bakker, former wife of a televangelist*
>
> *We used to build civilizations. Now we build shopping malls.*
>
> *—Bill Bryson, OBE, American British author*
>
> *Whoever said money can't buy happiness simply did not know where to go shopping.*
>
> *—Bo Derek, 10 actress and wife of the late American actor John Derek*

Moving

Jason Bourne is a fictional CIA assassin (created by Robert Ludlum) suffering from extreme memory loss. The original movie and subsequent series starred Matt Damon in the title role, except when he declined to do the fourth installment, in which Jeremy Renner took over the role when it was offered to him. Filmed partly in Manila, the scenes depicted a high intensity chase at EDSA, Epifanio delos Santos Avenue, where a few years back, the history of the Philippines was changed as the encampment of protest toppled the regime of what everyone thought of as a corrupt president. Pressured for reading the script for two hours before signifying his acceptance for the role, he had difficulty accepting some of the top-secret rules that accompanied the *Bourne Legacy* script. While not considered a reboot but a sequel to the franchise, the movie generated a modest enthusiasm and success worldwide.

EDSA was not what it is today when I left the country nearly five decades ago. It was called Highway 54, the number affixed to the former avenue (Avenida 19 de Junio) was mistakenly thought to represent the length in kilometers. It was later corrected to its present length of 23.8 kilometers. It was a strip lightly traveled, bounded generally by cogon grass on each side with few buildings interspersed, and it stretched from Monumento to Baclaran. Nowadays, it is teeming with all sorts of vehicles and cars, skyscrapers and malls on both sides, monorails above the streets, and it represents five decades of progressive decadence. Mention traffic in the city, and EDSA is always a poster for it. It was where the excitement of the chase in the Bourne sequel seemed to have mostly occurred.

Clutching the important documents, including an oversized envelope of my chest X-ray denoting I was not a medical liability, I took the step to a waiting Pan-Am plane to the United States in 1971. Together with me was my wife of two weeks as we traveled to a strange new land called New York City, USA. We became part of the less than 4 percent of legal immigrants from abroad, which at that time had deportable illegal immigrants from other countries numbering 345,353. It was the goal of almost everyone in my profession that specialization in a field of medicine was a must and the place to have postgraduate training was the United States. Thus, the eastern part of the United States, where most foreign-born arrivals gravitate, became a melting pot of people who moved from other parts of the globe, starting with the first Europeans around 1600 and Africans beginning in 1619. Both my wife and I spent our residency and postgraduate fellowship in medical schools and medical centers in the city.

While moving from the other side of the world to another in furtherance of postgraduate education, we resolved to return to our country of origin, where the customs and mores are native to our cultural makeup. This determination was drastically changed by the political upheaval, later a threat of revolution that made us change our minds and decide to seek our fortunes in the land of opportunity. Living in the city was acclimatization to the idea that one does not particularly care whether one knows the names of the neighbors in one's apartment. It was not that important in the rush of daily living. Parking on the streets was always a chore, as no matter what the season was, one had to move one's car from one side of the street to the other on the days the street sweeper came, else a traffic ticket with stiff fines was strapped between your car's windshield and wiper blades.

But life in a city that never sleeps has its own advantages, all interesting culturally, socially especially as ethnic diversity is an ever-present tapestry. People of different colors, origins, and backgrounds, some with clipped accents difficult to understand in communicating their newfound English language, were some of the patients that presented to the emergency rooms and hospital wards where we laid our hands on, percussed and listened to the chest with an ever-present stethoscope and many times opened their cavities with the slice of a scalpel. Museums and galleries became a diversion on weekends that were free; celebrities walking the crowded avenues were sometimes sighted despite trying to remain anonymous or incognito. But most of all, living in a metropolis of eight million people afforded us the training and specialization that caused us to move from the other side of the globe.

America's medical manpower was not a seasonal job at the time we finished our postgraduate education. Scouring the whole breath of the country to settle and practice the craft was basically a crapshoot and a feeling of uncertainty. This much was certain though: despite the lure of staying in the city and planting the roots that could have resulted in a favorable career outcome, we were adamant to leave New York City for other opportunities now that legal immigration did not count us out, coming from a country with one of the least immigrant population. The US Census Bureau, which was formed July 1, 1902, and started tackling the moving rate since 1948, came up with 35.5 million Americans move each year for a variety of reasons. We were moving, as AmericanMover.org indicates, part of the 9.9 percent of people relocating for a new job primarily and for other unspecified reasons such as closer to work or an easier commute, and most of all, practice opportunities.

There is a town in West Texas Panhandle that is as wide as ranches and farmlands stretch to the horizon. In it was littered with those grasshoppers better known as oil pumps in county patches dotted as well with gas wells. The town was also the home of the second largest refinery of Philips 66 in the state where the mesh called Marlex was developed. Even though the population of Hutchinson county was sparse compared to cosmopolitan New York City, it was where we settled, driving from east to west after packing in boxes the little appurtenances we had accumulated for the seven years of apartment living. Texas was not at that time the top 10 states that people move to but the opportunity of a hand surgeon, the idea of open skies and non-congested highways and a place to raise the two children born in the city beckoned. For those that asked what brought us to the far reaches of Texas, to a town where only three foreign families had recently moved from Ohio and Pennsylvania, the reasons we gave were not compelling enough. Initially, the nine American-educated, native-born, and Southwest-bred physicians steeped in the ways of their practice and referral patterns to specialists in a nearby city, were less accommodating to younger foreign-born colleagues, much less fully trained in the East Coast, which secretly I assumed was anathema to most, if not all of them. It took years of persistence and proving that we were not competition that eventually warmed them up. The only assurances I brought from the city were the telephone numbers and the promise of an answer to a consultation from a neophyte like me from my former attendings. The inhibitions and uncertainty of whether one would be accepted as a productive member of a community evaporated gradually with being enmeshed prominently in the social, political, and cultural life of a little town that at one time was dubbed an All-American City.

Thirty-eight years later, after a productive life in Borger, Texas, we hung up our gloves. A new hospital was built on the fringes of town, newer practitioners seeing the virtue of raising a family in a smaller town instead of relocating or staying in a big city and mindful of the glass ceiling—if ever there was one—created by the seniority we had established in the community, the new versus the old, the departures of old friends and colleagues made us hesitatingly move and relocate to another place. Whether we were part of the 2017 census statistic of 11 percent lowest moving rate, I hasten to add that we plied the I-40 interstate five years ago for the move. The boxes of anything we had accumulated—except for a few—were dutifully labeled, remaining unopened after five years. Stored in storage areas for a while until a place was built in a garage three years ago, they would probably remain unopened.

Moving is an exercise that is a part of American culture. It is said that in a life of a professional, the average move is about five times. If this is a yardstick we have to measure ourselves against, we have underperformed. But we still consider ourselves Texans.

> *We leave something of ourselves behind when we leave a place, we stay there, even though we go away. And there are things in us that we can find again only by going back there.*
>
> *—Pascal Mercier, Swiss writer and philosopher (pseudonym of Peter Bieri)*
>
> *A goodbye is never painful unless you're never going to say hello again.*
>
> *—Unknown*

Aging

A person once said that when given the choice of three situations he is confronted with, he would rather sit in front in a bus, drive in the middle of the street, and be in the back of a church. I do recall his preferential statements, which I have adopted as well because they are closest to what I will do in the face of the choices given. I am not a Pharisee but a publican in my approach to things like these, but I am fully aware that it is not all the time possible to do the two things he or I wish. The only thing that I can always do is stay at the back of a church on weekends or holy days of obligation when I go to the house of worship. No one calls you for transgression for the choice you made. Besides, because I literally know what comes next during the pastor's solemn recitation of the rites, sitting or standing at the back gives me a vantage view of those in front of me. And mostly, I see a sea of older folks with heads of black hair, even those younger ones who have shiny coronal occiputs but have remnants on their temporal sides. The younger generation who happen to join the sea of black plumes I don't mind. But those that try and attempt to perpetuate youth by coloring their hair black remind me of the same crowd I encounter at salons or barber shops when I go there to have my hair trimmed. They have their thinning mane dyed black or a slight variation thereof in an effort, I suppose, to defy their age and look younger when attending social functions or going to church. I do not consider the activity vanity because at one time, I attempted to have my graying hair done, when the colorist and I found out I was allergic to the dye and the procedure, what with my scalp interminably itchy and my face puffy. Since then, I decided to stick with the gray that interspersed with the remainder of the black hair I have. And so does my wife, who found out that the beautifully dyed and coiffed hair she had one time resulted in clumps of strands in her comb afterward. So now she does not even highlight her hair with L'Oreal.

The preoccupation with staying young and slowing down the aging process has taken both men and women to the many ways, sometimes to the extremes, recommended by many to achieve this end. It all starts with keeping the skin hydrated, taut, devoid of wrinkles, and retaining its youthful elasticity. To these exhortations are thousands of steps and ways to bring this about and stop or delay the ravages brought about by staying at the beach, tanning salon and the onslaught of changes brought by the number of years you live. Some involve cosmetic and permanent changes, others temporary. Some necessitate dietary restrictions, others intake of supplements and potions never heard of or used. A return to nature and the misgivings alluded to it in the past have resurfaced to justify the end but not always the means.

Which brings me to my good friend, John, a retired doctor and Air Force guy. We were killing time one afternoon at a Las Vegas premium outlet while waiting for our wives, who found the prices at the different shops alluring. John was eighty-three years old, in good shape, and unpretentious with his smile, and he almost always gave in to his wife's inclinations. A young woman who was probably not yet born during the Vietnam War, with nondescript tattoos all over her exposed limbs approached us and wanted to demonstrate how the wrinkles on one side of our face can be immediately removed by the application of the lotion she held in her hand. Having been subjected in the past to promotions of the concoction and not allowing myself anymore to be a part of the charade, I encouraged John to try, to which he reluctantly obliged, and she happily did. After a few minutes, the groove from where the wrinkles were, became shallower and disappeared. She made it clear, however, that the effects were just temporary and not permanent and for John to make the lines on his face and forehead disappear, he had to apply the lotion on a regular basis, especially if he had some social functions to attend to where age is bound to be a topic of conversation. But in the end, despite the sales pitch of the woman and, eventually, her supervisor, John and I were convinced that we would just retain our wrinkles, convincing ourselves like that old actor who says at the end of his sales pitch that we earned them.

Aging and its cause, up to now, remain uncertain. It does involve changes in a person's lifetime including physical, social, and psychological characteristics. It has been attributed, at some point, to DNA and the changes accumulated over time. It is known to slow down reaction time in human beings compared to the young. But older people are thought to be more knowledgeable about current events, about what is happening and what has happened in their surroundings than those who call themselves millennials. A 1934 experiment that increased the lifespan of rats, not humans, by 50 percent gave impetus to subsequent research that delayed or prevented aging. Out of the many studies that followed came the many recommendations about how to delay or prevent looking old. Pure coffee powder mixed with honey applied to the face, massage followed by warm water rinse, toner and moisturizer for hydrating and keeping the skin radiant, nutritional supplements, and many more are designed to defy the aging process.

There are many steps to keep age at bay; however, one can't hide some signs of aging, despite the skin glow and dyed black hair. Consider the sounds of worn-out and desiccated cartilage of a knee joint necessitating a walking aid, the opacity of a cataract that invades the lenses of the eye, the stooped posture and sometimes emaciated appearance and a loss of weight from an illness associated with years we can't defy. I may not have all the objective signs and symptoms of my age, but my hair is mostly gray and anybody who sits in the back probably can identify me from the sea of mostly black-haired supplicants in the front pews of a church.

Dining

Mention the alphabet aggrupation CIA, and the initials conjure a clandestine organization that is charged with protecting and preserving the interests of the United States all around the globe. Founded on July 26, 1947, when President Harry Truman signed the National Security Act, its forerunner was the Office of Strategic Services during World War II and the need to continue with foreign intelligence of the federal government, the information it gathers now is routinely given primarily to the president of the United States and the Cabinet. Though it uses human intelligence in gathering, processing, and analyzing national security information around the world, it nevertheless does not have a domestic security service, which is relegated to another government agency, the Federal Bureau of Investigation. The structure of the intelligence community has been modified since the September 11, 2011, event so that the CIA now reports to the Director of National Intelligence. To join and be a bona fide member of this organization requires undergoing a rigorous process that could last for a year or longer. One must be a citizen of this country, highly educated (with a college degree), should be eighteen but not over thirty-five years of age, interested in international affairs, and most of all, able to write clear and accurate reports that one has to submit. The tricks of the trade are learned at the compound of the agency vicariously baptized as The Farm.

But it was not the George Bush Center CIA campus in Langley, Virginia, we were at some years ago. It was another CIA, in the

Napa Valley area in California, part of the three-campus area in the United States of an institution that shares the same mnemonic but is otherwise called the Culinary Institute of America. The other international branch of this epicurean school is in Singapore. We were at the Greystone Cellars, a CIA campus in St. Helena, California, part of a tour group that descended on a hot summer day, in the northern part of the state known for clusters of vineyards and restaurants. Built in 1889 for a gentleman by the name of William Bowers, this 117,000-square-foot facility changed hands several times until the Christian Brothers converted the monastery-like campus into a winery with a well-known label from 1945 to 1989. It was acquired by the school in 1993 and has since become a mecca of people inquisitive and interested enough to know how to become purveyors of gastronomic art. On that particular day, forty of us were at the school's third floor in a glass-encased decury, observing how different menus were prepared, how a sous chef acting as second in command instructed the chefs de parte, commis chef, and even the kitchen porter on the finer points of serving discriminating diners. I was later told that those who participated in the kitchen were already professionals in their own right, matriculated for the event but saw the need for some more experience to hone their skills. They all came from around the country for the postgraduate course. It was all interesting to know how it is done in a premier school of culinary arts, but even though the school produced notable alumni—like Anthony Bourdain—who went on to be executive chefs in well-known restaurants in the country and other worldwide venues, I found out that there are lesser-known cooking schools that churned out respectable chefs whose creative spirit and culinary prowess I have later on sampled, like the son of my friend, who went on to be the executive chef of a well-known bistro in a major cosmopolitan city.

To let everyone know that I have been to a CIA institution, but not of the clandestine agent variety, I bought all the appurtenances of a chef's uniform that I intended to wear once I sauntered into our kitchen. This included the toque blanche, the characteristic white hat worn by a real cooking master, the double-breasted jacket, the pants, and the apron that identified me as the chef du jour. Of course, I did not wear the garb after I took it home, but after a year or two, I was generous enough to give all of it to a relative whose passion for the kitchen surpassed my desire and ability to compete with him.

The impetus for the subsequent popularity of gurus that now grace the screens the moment we turn on the television did not come as a surprise to me and, I suppose, to most of us. It was a future logical extension of what I thought we saw and experienced that day we drove to Napa Valley after a weeklong surgical conference in San Francisco. It has later made celebrities of Emeril Lagasse, Gordon Ramsay, Wolfgang Puck, Giada, Rachael Ray, and many others whose restaurants are all scattered in different cosmopolitan cities require almost mandatory reservations to be able to dine in. Many of their kitchen utensil endorsements appear in top of the line department stores. Shows like *Chopped* continuously air in several venues. I am not sure, though, whether these culinary personalities have stepped on the grounds or learned their craft from a venerable institution like the CIA, the Culinary Institute of America, which bills itself as a nonprofit provider of the best culinary education in the world.

I don't necessarily go to Michelin-starred restaurants if ever I go out. Or wade my way through CIA-alumni-led dining places to enhance my culinary experience. My tastes are simple enough, especially as I am made aware of the pictures of children particularly in Africa suffering from malnutrition and kwashiorkor, making me feel a pang of guilt courtesy of my late mother-in-law every time a morsel of food is left on my plate. I am also aware that 25 percent of food is wasted daily, considered garbage at the end of a business day and not given to or distributed to the crew of the restaurant because of legal restrictions imposed by health authorities. There have been some groups or outfits that are in the process of solving what they need to do to obviate this everyday wastage without running afoul of the existing laws. "To go" is a phrase I learned from many friends who find the excess food they ordered worth a second pass at home.

My brother Fred, however, finds that these are left forgotten in the fridge that many weeks later "to go" becomes a "specimen" that he throws away.

Retirement brings palatable choices such as to cook at home or go out to eat, especially now that there are only two people involved in the decision process. The choice is sometimes made lopsided by the vouchers given by casinos and restaurants for a free dinner, the ethnic and international flavors of cooking that abound, and the ease of sitting down before the dining table, not dressed up for a called-in reservation. We always check though every Wednesday at eleven o'clock in the evening a TV program called *Dirty Dining* disclosing which eating places we have to avoid, especially looking at all the pictures violating the mandates of health authorities.

An Indian friend and classmate from Trenton, New Jersey, while attending a business school in Florida at the turn of the century, insisted that the origin of culinary arts was in his home country and the spice trade, as it was known then, always led to the Orient. The Chinese have a different view. But I am not going to insinuate myself into this debate. I will just say that no matter what, a diploma from a world-renowned institution such as the Culinary Institute of America or CIA, if it is preferred to be called that way, while impressive to hold, does not always guarantee the approval of my discriminating palate and taste buds.

Wine Tasting

I have often been invited in the past to a wine-tasting event. I often have not heard of the sponsoring organizations except on some occasions by a group of enthusiasts at a country club I belong to. Neither did I know how they got my name and the fact that they culled me from their list as a connoisseur of wine. Of course, I am not and did not even consider myself as knowledgeable about wine. The only lists I have in my armamentarium was knowing whether it was a red or white and a couple of names or brands under each category. I showed up at these events, more often than not, to be polite—first, to respond to what I know was a gaffe by those that thought I was a wine lover, and second, to learn how to tell which among the wines scheduled for tasting, generally five varieties, defy my pretensions. I always ended up at the end of the line where dump buckets and crackers ended the experience, nodding in approbation about the wines tasted, simulating the judgment of those whom I thought knew what the assessment was all about. This much I can say: I will never host my own wine-tasting event.

Wine is grape juice fermented with yeast, a one-celled organism. Its origin is replete with archaeological evidence as early as the seventh century BC in China, to Greece, Italy, Armenia, and other sites of antiquity including ancient Egypt and Persia. Its use as a religious vehicle by some (forbidden for production and consumption by Islamic religion), festive celebratory occasions bordering on debauchery, medicinal and subsequent industrial purposes were some of the reasons that this consciousness-altering liquid burgeoned from its earliest beginnings to a favored offering to sovereigns of the medieval period. The Roman Empire's immense impact on the science of wine making and production and the development of the social norm affiliated with drinking can't be overemphasized, as they were the first to suggest that certain regions in Europe produced definitely superior wines, precursors of today's appellations became standard, notably these days from the Bordeaux region of France. Until recently, wines of Europe were considered superior to those of the Americas and other countries like New Zealand, Australia, South Africa, and South America, countries that do not have wine tradition. The latter half of the century changed this perception when favorable reviews were garnered in 1976 by American winemakers at the Paris wine tasting. That was when countries from the so-called New World began to gain respect. It is now more of a myth than a reality that the more expensive the wine is, the better it tastes than the inexpensive ones. While the quality of wine taste to my mind is more subjective than objective, wine connoisseurs are out to prove to the fallacy of this assumption.

Once in a while, to appear cultured and sophisticated, my wife and I spend an evening dining in a fancy restaurant, infrequently, if I may say so. There at a corner table with subdued lights, one can easily discern the presence of a wine glass together with another, ostensibly for bottled water. A sommelier with a tastevin vessel hanging over his or her neck comes in and after a few pleasantries recommends a wine paired with whatever food we order. My palate has never developed the ability to recall any wines except as to whether they are red or white. But deciding on the color of the spirits, I go through the required four steps of tasting the wine although I would rather have it poured outright. I am not into the anatomy or which part or side of my tongue or taste buds touches or perceives the texture of the wine. Neither are the senses that are ordinarily employed in the basic steps of wine tasting. I pretend to check the color and opacity of the wine, the aroma that frequently results in frustration, as I cannot make out whether the smell was derived from fruit or herbs or florals. Swirling and smelling, exposing the surface to a larger surface area even for a second, holding the glass by the stem and not by the bowl so as not to raise the temperature do not make any difference in the varietal I chose. In other words, the pretensions of sophistication are just that. I believe that the majority of those that go to these restaurants and go through the motions that I just described do so not because they are steeped in the art of wine tasting but to adhere blindly to common practice and what is expected of them.

Exploring the evolution of the science of viticulture and oenology involves knowing how grapes are fermented, the flavor engendered by the type or variety of grapes, the climate and the soil from where they are grown, the sugar and ethyl alcohol and the tannin content and whether the grapes are distilled in oak barrels, the pH of the distillate and how long the distillation process is, has become more complicated than summarizing the steps of the first open cholecystectomy in 1882 by a German surgeon named Carl Langenbuch. It was more than three decades earlier that Nathaniel Rothschild started his long association with the wine industry, following his purchase of a vineyard in Bordeaux, France. Five of the most expensive wines were sold by the Rothschilds, some ranging from $114,000 to $500,000 spanning the seventeenth to the twentieth century. What happened after these prize bottles were bought remained a conjecture. It is thought, however, that most are left unopened and part of an expensive collection. A story appeared many years ago, though, that someone in the possession of a premier crus was challenged and goaded eventually to open the precious bottle, only to find out that age had transformed the Chateau Lafite into an expensive vinegar. With time, white wines naturally darken, while reds begin to turn brown. I also learned that whites are best served with the temperature less than fifty-five degrees while reds are better with temperature more than fifty-five degrees Fahrenheit.

There must be an air of aristocracy for someone that has and tends to a vineyard. The distance between the stalks of grapes planted, the height and the trimming of the trees, the straight rows formed are like braided cornrows seen in some women's hairstyle. Among the many facets of wine tasting I have not learned, nor do I probably care to learn, is the type and shape of glass a wine is poured into. I will drink from whatever glass there is. Complicated to be a vintner and all the intricacies of wine and its characteristics, I would rather simply know how long an open wine bottle lasts.

Except when I am invited to a wine-tasting event or when I dine at a fancy restaurant.

House

Owning a house is one of the components of what everyone calls an American dream. It is what we aspire to own, for the family, a place to live in and build memories growing up. It is also a financial investment that builds equity and provides security for a future. A house, though its definition is different to most people, becomes a home when you feel comfortable providing more of a shelter at the end of a day. For many people, it is also a status symbol, a measure of what you have become. The size of the house, where it is located, the number of houses one owns speak of an aspect a society that defers to what you possess materially. It is tangible, and people like whatever they can see. Although these factors play a role in how some people need to be viewed and the opportunities that evolve from owning a house or houses, the cultural implications and beliefs of the diverse population in other countries still constitute a major consideration and differences in a house ownership. Values in Western countries, which focus on personal privacy and the formation of nuclear rather than a stem family, significantly affect the preferences that exist among adult children demands regarding housing needs.

Among the Asian-American population, the tradition of filial piety exists among the children. It resonates when adult children capable economically of owning a house decide as to whether to start with a nuclear or stem family. While it is a necessary obligation that children help their older parents with everyday life and thus form a stem family, many are beginning to adopt the Western style of a nuclear family, that is, to be separate and independent. This is particularly true among those that are well educated and inclined to start a living arrangement different from a co-residence model. This intergenerational living arrangement in owning a house, however, becomes reversed if the parents belong to higher socioeconomic status than those of their children. Because they are able to provide a better dwelling than their children, the likelihood of parents' ownership becomes greater. This traditional cultural ideology is evident when one walks through a house, especially that of a Chinese family, that includes additional rooms and other living arrangements of another family, generally the eldest son or daughter. Seldom can anyone in this Oriental tradition find the elder parents left alone in the present nursing home bereft of the demands of their children's housing need.

I thought that this tradition is only prevalent among the Asian culture. Owning a house is a universal ambition, but I am convinced now that economics plays a major role in preferences between generations and the personal needs of persons involved. Driving along the dusty streets of rainless Egyptian countryside on the way to the different antiquities of a civilization still preserved despite several centuries past, I saw on each side of the roads buildings two to four stories high, built like matchsticks of hollow blocks or bricks, the topmost floor with steel rebars on skinny concrete posts pointing to the sky. The visual images almost extended to not only the countryside but to the boulevards and streets of Cairo. Asked about the seemingly unfinished construction, the tour guide indicated that the unfinished topmost floors we saw with the steel rebars and the four-sided skinny post were designed and left that way for the older children to add and build on whenever they are able to afford to or when they return from where they are able to eke a living. It does not help to know that unemployment rate in this North African country stands presently at 33 percent. The scenes remind me of the ones I saw in my Middle East trips sometime back.

In the West, owning a house has brought in several concepts about the idea which started as a simple afterthought. People have to be reminded most of the time that owning a home is a resource that one can always turn to when one's financial needs are on the ropes. It is a financial investment, especially when mortgage used to finance it is far away from the original thirty- or fifteen-year loan. The equity will even be substantial if the house is paid for. Innovations regarding houses have also generated opportunities for most people owning a piece of Americana. Witness the emergence of reverse mortgage and the celebrities who are asked to peddle the advantages of the concept to those who waver at house ownership and the payments they still have to make. The pitches of Tom Selleck, Henry Winkler, and the late Fred Thompson resonate with many of the seniors who sometimes are faced with foreclosure to their homes and therefore could easily be victims of scam artists. That is not to say that reverse mortgages by well-intentioned companies are not a way of resolving some problems associated with owning a house, because they are. However, there is the problem of not totally owning a house or losing one. Mostly people in this category are down and out, or they resort to alcohol and drugs. Some are deprived of a fortune they once had because of unfortunate events in their lives. It would be easy to be judgmental when these homeless people encountered in big cities and suburban areas, living and relieving themselves in the streets and causing blight to and a problem in a city unable to cope with the social stigma. San Francisco or Seattle in the western part of the country are examples of this burgeoning decadence. Seldom is this seen or encountered where the elderly are taken in and cared for in a culture of intergenerational support, which is still a unique tradition of families in Eastern countries.

There is a happy medium for people, especially in the Western countries, who have owned their house for some time and have moved away from the stem or nuclear family structure. These are retirees like me, who, in the twilight of their lives, want to be independent of their children and grandchildren, having time left for themselves and having a bucket list still to accomplish while they can. It is called downsizing. It takes on several forms, such as moving out from a big and palatial residence to a much smaller house, a condominium, or an apartment, securing common but private living arrangements, having in place estate planning that does not include a trip to a nursing home. Insurance companies came up with the idea of long-term care assisted by a home care specialist when one becomes physically handicapped to do activities of daily living. While this is expensive to some, it does not deter the peace of mind to those who eventually include the policy together with the houses they own.

A house is not a home, some say. But a house provides a roof over your head when the rain falls. I would rather be dry than wet on a rainy day.

Birthdays

Growing up in a small village was not as complicated as it is many years later. Remembering the day when school opens, the flag-raising ceremony at a given time in the morning before class starts and the lowering in the afternoon to signify the class day is over were simple things every schoolchild remembers. Significant holidays when school doors were locked always provoked different reactions: those who did not want any break in the spontaneity of smooth sailing and rejected the interruptions imposed by the observance of the holiday, and those that welcomed the break after a few days of school activities. In my class, there were only a few things that we memorized or remembered then: when school began, the few holidays we were off from school, the three-month vacation time in summer before the new school calendar started again, and a few days in December like the fiesta in our village, when everyone employed elsewhere returned home to enjoy the festivities. We had only three schoolteachers, occasionally four, in the grade school so we knew beforehand who we were going to deal with for the rest of the coming school year. No one as far as I can recall had a calendar book or kept one to indelibly schedule the days and dates of these activities. Going to high school was just about the same as far as keeping tabs on the notable days of the year. College and going to the big city was a little different. The many activities to get involved in, though I seldom participated in many of them, required a bit more scheduling, so I began to keep track of the days and hours I selected to be a participant in the student group activities. I used the old-fashioned calendar in a notebook, which kept me in uncompromising stead for all the years I spent toward my eventual graduation from the university I attended.

I keep track of my daily schedule up to now, with the newer technology available. The many personal digital assistants I use compartmentalize every hour or minutes of the day that my mood changes from day to night if someone breaks the schedule I have for the day by unannounced visit, drop-in, calls for something not expected. It is being inflexible all right, but sanity sometimes requires rigidity in a discipline developed and accustomed to. This is true in my years of surgical practice and the life I live nowadays. Even in retirement, I overload my smartphone with birthdays, anniversaries, vacations, important holidays, names of husbands, family relatives, social obligations, and many more, but I could not, for the life of me, figure out how my late mother could remember the birthdays and the accompanying details of us and her twenty-eight grandchildren then without notes when we had our first family reunion in 1990. I am not sure that she would be able to these days if she were alive, now that there are more than fifty or sixty grandchildren in the family tree. I suppose mothers are imbued with a certain gift of memory that tells them when they finally discharge from their womb what they carried for nine months. And as extension of their special gift, the exact days when the children of their children begin the lives they are given.

Birthdays are a beginning. A birthday is a momentous occasion whose importance cannot be overstated. Every year that we commemorate the day each of us was born and given a chance to fulfill whatever mission, unique or simple, is a time to celebrate and, at the same time, reflect on ourselves and the society we are in. True that we generally mark another year of existence with parties and cakes to continue with what the Greeks started many centuries ago to honor Artemis, the goddess of the moon, letting the lit candles' smoke carry the prayers and wishes to the gods and the skies. But more than this, the indispensable day brings us a new beginning and a rebirth of how we are responding to the calling at the particular stage of our lives.

I still get the many birthday cards from friends and relatives alike, with the usually "happy birthday" quotes, written in longhand or signed after a Hallmark greeting. I get birthday gifts from a few, and for those that live close by, I still am obligated to take them out for lunch or dinner to show them how much I appreciate being alive for another year, which is what I am thankful for, the good luck looking forward to the next time this event happens. Whether it comes on the day of birth or a week before, I do not feel like the Germans, who consider it a bad luck to wish one a happy birthday before the actual date. Though it is becoming repetitive every year and the enthusiasm is not as anticipated as when one is still young, it is nevertheless a blessing to add another ring to the trunk and count it with family and friends.

I was born on December, which, like January and February, are the least common times in America to be born. It means, however, that based on data provided by the National Center for Health and Statistics and the Social Security Administration, it takes thirty-eight weeks for pregnancies to last, so I am convinced that I was conceived during the holidays, when many people plan on having a baby. Though I am not sure of how accurate my guess is and only my late mother can confirm this fact, I intend to be around longer in the years to come and not be just a snapshot in time.

Bookworm

I love to read. When I first learned how to read, I became a bookworm right away, spending most of my spare time enjoying the beginning and the end of a good story. Reference to the origin of the word in 1713 mentioned certain larvae of insects that made holes in the bindings and paper of a book. It was even mentioned earlier, in the fourteenth century, when libraries did not have the heating or air conditioning that exist today. Though the idea that some insects make their homes inside a book and thus the term *bookworm* was coined, it seldom is a problem nowadays because the glue used in binding newer and modern books has ingredients that bugs don't like. Older books, maybe so. I don't consider the term derogatory like some people do, equating a person reading more than the usual to be a beetle or a louse that burrows itself in a book. If one has to look at the list of those individuals who, growing up, frequented the small municipal library in our town to borrow books, I would probably top the list. It exposed me to a wide range of words I did not know even existed (like *wanderlust* or *petrichor*), a language I was still foreign to, improved my meager cognitive skills, concentration, and perception I needed in the profession I eventually chose. It is not limited to an individual who wants to improve his or her vocabulary and intelligence but to every person who finds the value of a printed page or the spoken word that exists in other medium variously called audiobooks.

There are now a number of ways one can avail oneself of being a reader or a true bookworm. Several mobile electronic devices, such as Kindle, Kobo, Oasis, or Fire, allow for easy portability of any book or magazine to download and read while on the move as when one is on a car, bus, or airplane. While I have two of these e-reader digital devices and have tried them to appear like a purveyor of something technologically savvy, I much prefer holding a thicker book in my hands even if it is cumbersome to carry it on a trip. Walk through the house, and every corner has stacks of at least two books I finish every week. The shelf in the library is all filled up. Being somewhat of a dedicated bibliophile, however, does not necessarily mean that I catalogue or organize the books I end up collecting. Locating or seeking a particular volume becomes a chore that is easily left mostly to chance.

Though collectively it is, to some, enjoyable to belong to a book club that meets regularly to read and discuss a particular book, I never was a part of this group. I have always preferred to start reading alone, sometimes borrowing reading time when the list on my schedule is less important or an appointment permits a little diversion. Finishing several chapters, especially if the story or the subject is interesting or mind-absorbing, makes me forget the time spent on a creative masterpiece. It is not like the short time spent on reading a blurb or a short promotional piece generally printed on the back of a book jacket, written by the author or publisher, or testimonials from other writers. I could not, however, finish in several sittings reading the one thousand one hundred eighteen chapters of the Old and New Testaments even if I tried.

Considering myself a bookworm, I wanted to accomplish one thing, however, aside from regularly entering Barnes and Noble, Walmart, Costco, and the like, to look for new titles of best sellers: to write a book. I do not possess the imagination of a good novelist like Baldacci, Turow, Berenson, or Daniel Silva. To tell a story that connects and is relatable to a reader is not a forte that I can count on. Entering a bookstore and knowing how many new books are published every week and competing against established or published writers diminishes any hope of developing whatever genre I need to identify, the focus and the coherence of a story an author needs to tell, and the research that most writers undertake to make the scenes in the book almost real. Submitting written material to the review of a literary editor, the sometimes endless disenchantment and frustration of being rejected by a publisher or a literary agent is always hard for someone writing, especially for the first time. Self-publishing has become the way for those who still look for the vicarious satisfaction of having their prose in print despite the process of submission and subsequent rejection by major publishing houses. In fact, self-publishing has captured and exploded to a record 38 percent of approximately eight hundred thousand printed books in 2017. It has even surprised the major publishers of a gem and bestseller that originally was turned down.

While I do not have the requisite traits of a good writer or author, such as focus on development of a story, discipline and clarity of an idea, fluency and word choice, and other qualities of writing or becoming an author of novels; a passion for reading, the love of words and writing common events with different slants or context probably are not enough to make me a Clancy or Deepak Chopra.

I think I will just remain a bookworm.

Insurance

I just bought another vehicle. It was not a spur-of-the-moment purchase, though it took a little while before I added another one to the five existing carriers in my garage and driveway. I have to call another of my brothers to give away one of my vehicles to make room for the new one, something that I have always done in the past because of my old habit of not selling an older model I have to get rid of but giving it away to a relative or sometimes donating it to charity. A friend of mine placed his hand on one side of my face as if to gauge whether I have the fever to walk in and out of showroom with another deal in hand. I incidentally did the same similar trick with him whenever he got another car from a dealership in town.

One of the very first must-do activities to lock up any deal was to call the insurance agent and make sure that insurance was attached to the purchase. This cambium contract has become a commonplace to anything we own or have, the idea of which is to eliminate, minimize, or spread the risk of the property we possess. It is a requirement of modern business, though the development of the history of insurance can be traced centuries back, practiced in many forms in societies and cultures engaged in monetary economies. And there are many types of insurance that have been spawned by an industry that eventually developed and saw the need of business conglomerates, people, or customers who shoulder the risk of having financial instruments such as the new SUV I just purchased. There are property, business, accident, life, and all sorts of other forms of protective enterprise offered to the public, regulated by laws and restrictions promulgated these days by the government.

Risk-taking or aversion thereof has always been part of the equation in asset preservation as practiced by the Chinese and Babylonian merchants in the third or second millennia BC, the latter traders recording their system in the Code of Hammurabi. To minimize the risk of total loss of a boat capsizing from rivers and rapids as merchants carrying the goods sailed the open waters, lenders charged them for the loans to finance the shipment. The high rate charged was condemned and decried by then Pope Gregory IX, resulting in modification of contracts, where both the venture capitalist and the traders became partners in the enterprise, both sharing the profits. Modern forms of insurance and specialized varieties then became more sophisticated and were invented. Thus, fire, life, accident, and property insurance and the like were developed later, based on actuarial and mathematical odds of underwriting these instruments.

Benjamin Franklin, he of the well-known lightning character and personality in colonial America, founded an insurance company in 1752, popularizing and contributing to avoiding the hazards associated with fire and standardizing insurance requirements during his time. It is not too often today, as we turn on our television, flip the pages of a newspaper or magazine, that we are lured into having, adding, or modifying the insurance that we have, all originating from ventures, guilds, and enterprise founded in ancient and medieval times as a result of some catastrophic events such as the loss of a ship or the Great Fire in London in 1666 that resulted in the loss of 13,000 homes and was the impetus for the founding of property insurance. Several names and groups as well as houses have been associated with the development of the industry, such as the Greeks and Romans, who introduced health and life insurance, the Persian monarchs who were responsible for some form of political insurance, and Hamburger Feuer, who formed the first fire insurance company in the world. It appears, though, that the English people originated most of the modern insurance policies we know them today, together with the mathematical and statistical tools associated with how the premiums are determined.

In some places, notably among Third World countries, where it is not mandated by the government to insure whatever property needs to be risk-averse or risk-free to own or possess them, people don't carry these instruments of life or property protection. In the small village where I originally came from, I do not know of anyone who has life or any form of insurance that one holds close to the vest. Life is what goes on, and people never looked back and regretted whatever unfortunate circumstance came along their way. Of course, in larger metropolis and in a more modern society, bundled or not, insurance requirements now have become part of estate planning, seen as a necessity by many and, on some property, required by regulatory authorities—my new vehicle included.

Whether we follow ancient, medieval, or modern beliefs, I find it antithetical that we go to church and pray to the good Lord, among other things, that we will always have the good fortune of being religious faithful and that we should avoid and be spared from the vicissitudes of life and yet we go out of the church and purchase insurance against what we have just prayed for. The dominance of insurance companies constantly reminds me many years ago, driving down East River highway in Manhattan as I went to work and seeing all the apartment and condominium complexes erected and owned by the insurance company that also had developed mathematically the table used by doctors as to what is an ideal weight for someone's height. It is standard medical practice still used today.

I often wonder that with the many types of insurance underwritten today and the proliferation of companies that now buy from you the insured to eliminate the problem of paying the premium, whether long- or short-term policies, the suspicion the hope is that they won't subsidize for long the benefits they assume for paying the premiums on your behalf. It does not mean that I impugn any ulterior motives to how they came to be structured. They altruism these companies have for their customers must be acknowledged as well. I have not had anyone pay for the benefits my estate would receive should

I not survive for a long time. Instead, I have terminated some of them, as the reasons for having them were erased gradually from my viewpoint. I just needed, however, an additional policy for the new vehicle I just added to what I already have in my garage.

Edward E. Quiros, MD, MBA, FACS, FICS, CMCM
2795 Culloden Avenue
Henderson, Nevada 89044
Phone: 702.776.8236
CP: 806.886.8249
E-mail: edqui@aol.com

EDUCATION

2004–2006:	Concord University School of Law
1999:	Master of Business Administration, University of South Florida, Tampa, Florida
1970:	Doctor of Medicine, University of Santo Tomas, Manila Philippines
1965:	Bachelor of Arts, University of Santo Tomas, Manila Philippines
1964:	Bachelor of Science, University of Santo Tomas, Manila Philippines

POSTGRADUATE MEDICAL EDUCATION

1969–1970:	USAF Hospital Clark, Rotating Internship
1970–1971:	USAF Hospital Clark, Residency, Internal Medicine
1971–1972:	City Hospital Center at Elmhurst/Mt. Sinai Hospital New York, NY, Surgical Internship
1972–1974:	New York Medical College Hospitals, NY, NY Resident, General Surgery
1974–1975:	New York Medical College Hospitals, NY, NY Senior Resident, General Surgery
1975–1976:	New York Medical College Hospitals, NY, NY Chief Resident, General Surgery
1976–1977:	New York Medical College Hospitals, NY, NY Fellow, Hand Surgery (Under Dr. Sylvester Carter)

BOARD CERTIFICATION

American Board of Surgery, certified in 1981, recertified in 1992, recertified in 2002
American Board of Managed Care Medicine, 2001
Texas Workmen's Compensation Board

LICENSURE

New York, 1974–1977
Texas, 1977–present
Philippines, license to expire 2022

PROFESSIONAL AFFILIATIONS/POSITIONS

1976–1977: Metropolitan Hospital Center, NY, NY Assistant Attending Surgeon
1976–1977: Midtown Hospital, NY, NY Associate Attending Surgeon
1977–2013: Golden Plains Community Hospital, Borger, Texas Attending Surgeon, General/ Hand and Upper Extremity
1972–1977: Hansford County Hospital, Spearman, Texas
1972–1978: Attending Surgeon, General/Hand and Upper Extremity
1988–2013: Memorial Hospital, Dumas, Texas Consultant in Hand and Upper Extremity Surgery
2002–2013: Pampa Regional Medical Center, Pampa, Texas Consultant in Hand and Upper Extremity Surgery

PROFESSIONAL ORGANIZATIONS

Fellow, American College of Surgeons
Fellow, International College of Surgeons
Fellow, American Society of Abdominal Surgeons

Fellow, Society of Philippine Surgeons in America
Member, Surgical Society of New York Medical College
Member, American Society of Contemporary Medicine
Member, New York Academy of Sciences
Member, American College of Physician Executives
Member, Top of Texas County Medical Society (Lifetime)
Member, Texas Medical Association (Lifetime)
Life Member, Vietnam Veterans of America

PROFESSIONAL and CIVIC POSITIONS

1979–1984: Board of Directors, Borger Country Club

- First non-Caucasian elected to the board. None has been elected since.

1980–1993: St. Johns Parish Council

- Organized the first Winterfest festival of the parish. It has continued since as a fundraiser for the parish and the parish school.
- Started the parish choir

1993–1996: Member, Amarillo Diocesan School Board

- Advised and recommended to the bishop and the superintendent on matters affecting the Catholic schools in the diocese.
- Revised Diocesan School Board Policy and procedures
- Develop marketing and promotional activities

1992–2013: Board of Regents, Frank Phillips College. Elected in 1992, Re-elected in 1994, Re-elected in 1996 (6-year term), Re- elected in 2002 and 2008 for another 6-year term.
(Resigned in 2013 when I retired from active practice)

- Subcommittee developed performance evaluation for college president and Board of Regents self-evaluation
- Helped developed the college's workforce Development Center and college off-campus branches to serve area-wide industries
- Participated in the study and implementation of the college's computer and information technology systems
- During stint on the board, worked with different organizations to build and expand college campuses in its ten-county area

1989–1994: Board of Directors, Hutchinson County Hospital District

- Ad hoc committee that worked for the passage of an enabling legislation by the Texas Legislature creating the hospital district
- As president of the board, established the hospital's pension system for its employees
- Leadership role in having the hospital accredited three times by JCAHO
- As one of the three members of the finance committee, oversaw the operations and the evaluated the financial performance of the hospital on a monthly basis

1994: Hutchinson County Ad Hoc Committee

- Committee delegated to present to the Texas Department of Criminal Justice the county's bid to have prison facilities built in Hutchinson County

1996–1997 President, Catholic Physicians Guild, Amarillo, Texas

- Led and presided over activities of all the Catholic physicians and dentists in the whole diocese of Amarillo.

Conducted several annual medical consultations especially for the nuns in the diocese.

1988, 1991–1992, 1996–1997: Delegate to the Texas Medical Association's House of Delegates

- Served on the Council on Scientific and Public Affairs that recommended resolutions brought to the floor of the House for discussion and adoption as policy matters.

1981–1983, 1997–1998: Chief of Staff, Golden Plains Community Hospital
1979–1987, 1994, 1999–2000: Chief of Surgery, Golden Plains Community Hospital

- Was actively involved in leadership role in three JCAHO accreditation processes for the hospital. As chief of surgery, was instrumental in obtaining ACS Trauma Designation for the hospital.

2002, 2003: President, Society of Philippine Surgeons in America

- First to hold the office of the president for two years in a row, was the society's executive secretary before becoming president.
- As a fellow of the society, has hosted several fully trained surgeons from the Philippines during their fellowship rotation as traveling fellow. Fellowship rotation included teaching, scrubbing and operating at the host's clinic, practice and hospital setting.

2000–present: Editor in chief, *Philippine Surgeon*, the official publication of the Society of Philippine Surgeons in America
2000–present: Website editor: spsatoday.com

2010–2013: Clinical professor of Surgery, Lincoln Memorial University College of Medicine, Tennessee

- Medical students rotate at my office and hospitals. Instructions given during their rotation; student clinical evaluation given to school at the end of their rotation.

2014–present: Co-chair, Surgical Missions Committee, Society of Philippine Surgeons in America

- During these surgical missions, local surgeons scrub and assist especially on hand cases to learn surgical procedures.
- Lectures given as part of educating surgeons at several mission sites.

Member in Different Local Civic and Political Organizations in Texas

Have presented papers and delivered talks and continue to be a speaker at surgical meetings and symposia locally, nationally, and internationally on Hand and Upper Extremity, General Surgery and on Management and Service Quality topics, including Medical Societies, Philippine College of Surgeons, USTMAA, USTMAAA, UST Faculty of Medicine and Surgery Department of Surgery; on the Faculty of Society of Philippine Surgeons in America's Surgical Symposia (Scheduled to be a CME speaker in May 2015 and the Society's 41st CME Surgical Symposium in July 2015)

Gave lectures on Scientific Topics sponsored by CME SPSA, 2016 and at recent 45th Anniversary and 43rd CME of SPSA, Las Vegas, Nevada August 2017.

AWARDS and RECOGNITIONS

- Best Surgeon, Hutchinson County 2011, *News-Herald Borger*
- Doctor of the Year, 2009, Golden Plains Community Hospital
- American Heart Association, 1991
- Certificate of Recognition, Golden Nail Awards, Amarillo, Texas
- Several certificates from USTMAA, UST Faculty of Medicine and Surgery, and Philippine College of Surgeons
- Awards and recognition from several governors, congressmen, and senators from the Republic of the Philippines

PERSONAL

Married to Corazon Panlilio-Quiros, MD (Obstetrician-Gynecologist)
Children: **Roderick Michael Quiros**, MD, Surgeon (Surgical Oncology), St. Luke's Medical Center, Bethlehem, PA; Clinical Associate Professor of Surgery, Temple University, College of Medicine, Philadelphia, PA
Christine Quiros, Analyst, Empire Bank, Manhattan, New York
Emily Mathis-Quiros, MD (Daughter-in-law) Pediatric Anesthesiologist, St. Christopher Children's
Hospital, Philadelphia, PA
Three grandchildren: Olivia Marie, Noemi, Isabelle Claire